HERSHEY'S®

CHOCOLATE
COOKBOOK

WEST
SIDE
PUBLISHING

West Side Publishing is a division of Publications International, Ltd.

© 2008 Publications International, Ltd.

Recipes and text © 2008 The Hershey Company. All recipe photography © Publications International, Ltd.

Louis Weber, CEO
Publications International, Ltd.
7373 North Cicero Avenue
Lincolnwood, IL 60712

Front and back cover photography and photography on pages 1, 3, 4-5, 6, 13, 27, 28, 43, 54, 69, 73, 75, 77, 85, 91, 95, 100, 103, 112, 113, 121, 125, 130, 143, 151, 154, 157, 159, 162, 179, 201, 202, 213, 216, 223, 235, 248, and 250 by Stephen Hamilton Photographics, Inc, Chicago.

Photographers: Tate Hunt, Jennifer Marx
Photographers' Assistant: Tony Favarula
Prop Stylist: Tom Hamilton
Food Stylists: Kathy Joy, Walter Moeller
Assistant Food Stylist: Jill Kaczanowski

Pictured on front cover: HERSHEY'S Lavish Chocolate Cake *(page 84)*.

Pictured on back cover (left to right): Chocolate Almond Torte *(page 94)*, Collector's Cocoa Cake *(page 74)*, and White & Chocolate Covered Strawberries *(page 212)*.

Pictured on back flap: All-Chocolate Boston Cream Pie *(page 124)*.

ISBN-13: 978-1-4127-2947-5
ISBN-10: 1-4127-2947-5

Manufactured in China.

8 7 6 5 4 3 2 1

FOR THE LOVE
OF CHOCOLATE

6   GETTING STARTED

12   DAZZLING
COOKIES & BITES

42   BOUNTIFUL
BROWNIES & BARS

72   CLASSIC CAKES

102   TASTY CHEESECAKES

120   ENTICING PIES & TARTS

158   TIMELESS TREATS
& DESSERTS

200   CREATIVE CANDIES
& SWEETS

222   SPECIAL OCCASIONS
& CELEBRATIONS

250   INDEX

GETTING STARTED

Baking Tips, Hints, and Guidance

Whether you are a novice or a baking expert, these tips are sure to come in handy for achieving the best overall outcome. We've included suggestions on selecting ingredients, baking hints, and troubleshooting—just in case a problem occurs. Read through our tips, hints, and guidance, and you'll be making delicious desserts in no time.

WORKING WITH INGREDIENTS
USING BUTTER, MARGARINE, AND SPREADS

Butter

Butter is made from fresh or soured cream and must contain at least 80% fat by law. The remaining 20% is composed of milk solids and water. For baking, ONLY use butter in the stick form. Whipped butter has air beaten into it and cannot be directly substituted for stick butter. The HERSHEY₀S Kitchens uses regular stick butter that contains salt in all recipe development and testing. Unsalted butter may be substituted for regular butter with little difference in the overall taste of the recipe.

Margarine

Margarine must contain 80% vegetable fat by law. It is often made from soybean, canola, and corn oils. Because margarine is made from vegetable oil, it contains less saturated fat than butter. For baking, ONLY use margarine in stick form. The softer margarine found in tubs may have air beaten in to it, which will negatively affect the outcome of your recipe. Margarine made with 80% fat is the only acceptable substitution for butter. Read package labels carefully. Many products will look like margarine, but they are actually spreads.

Spreads

Spreads contain less than 80% fat by weight. Water typically replaces the fat in spreads. DO NOT use spreads in baking unless a recipe calls for a specific type of spread. For example, $1/2$ cup 60% vegetable oil spread.

Reduced-Calorie or Low-Fat Butter or Margarine

These products have considerably less fat than regular butter or margarine and usually contain added water and air. Unless a recipe specifically lists these products, do not use them for baking, as poor quality and texture will occur.

USING CHOCOLATE AND COCOA

Storing Chocolate

Chocolate products will stay fresh for well over a year if stored in a cool, dry place (65–70°F.). It's a good idea to keep an eye on the temperature and humidity. Bloom, the gray-white film that sometimes appears on chocolate bars and chips, occurs when chocolate is exposed to varying temperatures. It does not affect the taste or quality of the chocolate.

MELTING CHOCOLATE

General Tips

- Choose a cool, dry day to melt chocolate for chocolate coating. Humidity in the air or even in the kitchen will cause chocolate to tighten up or become stiff and grainy, a condition known as "seizing."
- Use only very dry utensils when melting chocolate. Wet utensils (even with 2 or 3 drops of water) can cause chocolate to seize.
- Break chocolate into small pieces to speed the melting process.
- Chocolate can scorch easily. Stir melting chocolate periodically to help blending and discourage scorching.
- If during the melting process the chocolate product begins to tighten or become lumpy, you can add a small amount of solid vegetable shortening (not butter, margarine, spreads, oil, water or milk) to the chocolate, chocolate chips, chocolate squares or other baking pieces. Stir in 1 level tablespoon solid vegetable shortening for each 6 ounces of chocolate you are melting. Six ounces is equal to 1 cup baking chips or 6 (1-ounce) squares of baking chocolate.

Microwave Method

- Use only microwave-safe containers to melt chocolate in the microwave and place container with chocolate in the center of the microwave to melt.
- Handle microwave containers with a hot pad after heating. The container may be hotter than contents.
- Do not overheat; chocolate and other baking ingredients can scorch easily. Because of stronger microwaves on the market today, you may want to start with 50% power when melting chocolate.
- Baking chips and baking chocolate may appear formed and unmelted after heating but will become fluid after stirring.

Direct Heat Method

- When melting chocolate on a range or stovetop use very low heat, use a heavy saucepan, and stir constantly.

Double Boiler Method

- Place chocolate or other ingredients in double boiler top over hot, not boiling, water. Be careful, boiling water may cause steam droplets to get into chocolate which can result in "seizing," when the chocolate becomes stiff and grainy.

- Stir occasionally with a clean, dry utensil until the chocolate is melted.

Storing Cocoa

HERSHEY®S Cocoa keeps very well when stored at room temperature in the original container. It retains its freshness and quality without refrigeration.

When storing HERSHEY®S Cocoa, avoid contact with moisture and/or high heat. Both can cause clumping and gray discoloration, although neither affect cocoa flavor or quality.

Chocolate Substitutions

HERSHEY®S Cocoa can be used as an easy substitute for most forms of baking chocolate and even baking chips called for in recipes. Use the following chart as a guideline for your needs:

PRODUCT	COCOA	SHORTENING	SUGAR	AMOUNT
Unsweetened Baking Chocolate	3 Tbsp.	1 Tbsp.		Equals 1 oz. Scale up accordingly.
Pre-melted Unsweetened Baking Chocolate	3 Tbsp.	1 Tbsp.		Equals 1 envelope
Semi-Sweet Baking Chocolate	6 Tbsp.	¼ cup	7 Tbsp.	Equals 6 oz. Semi-Sweet or 1 cup Semi-Sweet Chocolate Chips
Sweet Baking Chocolate	3 Tbsp.	2⅔ Tbsp.	4½ Tbsp.	Equals 4 oz. bar

USING COCONUT

Toasting Coconut

- Heat oven to 350°F.
- Spread MOUNDS® Sweetened Coconut Flakes in a thin layer in a shallow baking pan.
- Bake 5 to 10 minutes, stirring occasionally, until light golden brown.

Storing Coconut

To store a bag of MOUNDS® Coconut after opening, tightly close the bag and place it in the refrigerator. You can also place the opened bag inside a heavy resealable plastic bag and store it in the freezer.

BAKING TIPS

CAKES

Selecting Bakeware

- Be sure to use the pan size called for in the recipe. To check the width of a pan, measure across the top from inside edge to inside edge.
- Use shiny metal pans for baking cakes. They reflect heat away, producing a tender, lighter-colored crust.
- Use caution when using dark nonstick baking pans or glass baking dishes. Read and follow the manufacturer's directions. Since these pans absorb more heat, results may be better if the baking temperature is reduced by 25°F.

Preparation

- Grease and/or flour pans as directed in recipes for butter-type cakes. Do not grease pans for angel, sponge, and chiffon cakes unless directed in the recipe.
- Fill cake pans no more than half-full to allow for rising during baking.

Baking/Cooling/Frosting

- Bake cakes with the oven rack placed in the center of the oven, unless the recipe states differently. Bake only on 1 rack.
- Cakes should be cooled completely on wire racks. Cool round cakes in their pans 10 minutes, then loosen and remove from pans to wire racks. Rectangular cakes (often in 13×9-inch baking pans) can be cooled completely in the pan or cooled 10 minutes in the pan and then removed to a wire rack to cool completely.
- Frost cakes when they are completely cooled, or the frosting will melt or slide off the cake.

Storage & Cutting

- Cool unfrosted cakes completely before storing, or they will become sticky on the surface.
- Store cakes with creamy frostings under a cake saver or large inverted bowl.
- Store cakes with whipped cream toppings, cream fillings, or cream cheese frostings in the refrigerator.

Troubleshooting

If a homemade cake has a coarse texture, the following problems may have occurred:

- Too much baking soda or baking powder may have been used.
- Not enough liquid may have been used.
- The butter and sugar may not have been beaten together long enough. If the recipe calls for creaming butter and sugar, or beating until light and fluffy, this should take at least 3 to 4 minutes of beating.
- The oven temperature was too low.

If a homemade cake is too dry, the following problems may have occurred:

- Too much flour or leavening (baking soda/baking powder) was used.
- Not enough shortening or sugar was used.
- The cake was over-baked—the oven temperature was too high and/or the baking time was too long.

If a homemade cake fell (the center of the cake sinks), the following problems may have occurred:

- The cake was under-baked—the oven temperature was too low and/or the baking time was too short.
- The liquid was over- or under-measured.
- The pan was too small—the batter was too deep.
- The cake was moved or jarred before it was sufficiently baked.
- Old or expired baking powder was used.
- A wooden pick or cake tester was inserted into the cake before it was sufficiently set.

If a homemade cake has low volume or is too flat, the following problems may have occurred:

- The liquid was over- or under-measured.
- The batter was under-mixed or extremely over-mixed.
- The pan was too large.
- The oven temperature was too low or too high.

If a homemade cake has a peaked center, the following problems may have occurred:

- The batter was over-mixed.
- The oven temperature was too hot.

If a homemade cake shrinks excessively around the edges, the following problems may have occurred:

- The baking pans were greased too heavily.
- The baking pans were placed too close together in the oven.
- There was too little batter in the baking pan.
- The batter was extremely over-mixed.
- There was too little liquid in the batter.
- The cake was over-baked—either too long a time or at too high a temperature.

If a homemade cake is soggy, the following problems may have occurred:

- The cake was moved or jarred before it was sufficiently baked.
- The cake was under-baked—the oven temperature was too low and/or the baking time was too short.
- Old or expired baking powder was used.

If a homemade cake has a spotted crust, the batter was probably under-mixed.

If a homemade cake has a sticky top crust, the following problems may have occurred:

- The cake was stored while still warm.
- The liquid was over-measured.

- The cake was under-baked—the oven temperature was too low and/or the baking time was too short.
- The air humidity was too high.

If a homemade cake has tunnels throughout the layer, the following problems may have occurred:

- The oven temperature was too high.
- The batter was under-mixed or extremely over-mixed.

If a homemade cake has uneven browning, the following problems may have occurred:

- There was uneven heat circulation in the oven.
- The baking pans were placed too close together in the oven.

CHEESECAKES

Selecting Bakeware

A springform pan (with removable side and bottom) is the most commonly used pan for making cheesecakes.

Preparation

Avoid over-beating the batter. Over-beating incorporates additional air and tends to cause cracking on the surface of the cheesecake. For even marbling and the best distribution of added ingredients, such as chocolate chips or nuts, do not over-soften or over-beat the cream cheese.

Baking/Cooling

- Avoid over-baking.
- Cheesecake baking times are not always exact, due to variations in ovens. The cheesecake will continue to bake after it is removed from the oven. The center of the cheesecake should be just slightly moist when it is ready to be removed.
- Upon removal from the oven, loosen the cake from the edge of the pan by running the tip of a knife or narrow spatula between the top edge of the cake and the side of the pan. This allows the cake to pull away freely from the pan as it cools.

- Cool the cheesecake on a wire rack away from drafts.
- After a cheesecake has cooled completely, gently loosen the entire side of the cheesecake from the pan with the tip of a knife while slowly releasing the springform pan clamp. Carefully remove the side of the pan.

Storing

- Baked cheesecakes freeze well. Cool them completely and wrap them securely in heavy-duty foil or plastic wrap, but do not freeze cheesecakes with garnishes or toppings.

COOKIES

Selecting Bakeware

- Use a shiny, flat cookie sheet at least 2 inches narrower and shorter than your oven rack. The cookie sheet may be open on 1, 2, or 3 sides. Cookies may not brown evenly if a cookie sheet is warped.
- Follow manufacturer's instructions if using a cookie sheet with a nonstick coating; the oven temperature may need to be reduced by 25°F.
- Follow manufacturer's instructions if using an "insulated" cookie sheet; cookies may take slightly longer to bake or may brown differently.

Preparation

- Grease the cookie sheet only if directed in the recipe, using solid vegetable shortening (not butter, margarine, vegetable oil, spread, or oil) or use nonstick cooking spray.
- Make cookies the same size and thickness to ensure uniform baking.
- Clean and cool cookie sheets before reusing or cookies may stick to sheet or spread too much.
- Always be sure to remove the foil wrapping from HERSHEY'S KISSES® BRAND Chocolates before placing them on cookies. Do not put cookies back into the oven after placing chocolates on top of them. Do not substitute HERSHEY'S KISSES® BRAND with Almonds for HERSHEY'S KISSES® BRAND Chocolates, as they may melt too much from the heat of the cookies.

Baking/Cooling

- Bake only 1 sheet of cookies at a time in the center of the oven.
- Check cookies at minimum baking time.
- Remove baked cookies immediately from the cookie sheet with a wide spatula, unless the recipe states other cooling directions. Place cookies in a single layer on a wire rack to cool completely before storing.

Storing

- Store crisp, thin cookies in a container or a tin with a loose-fitting cover.
- Store unfrosted soft cookies in an airtight container to preserve moistness.
- Store frosted soft cookies in a single layer in an airtight container so that the frosting will maintain its shape and the cookies will remain moist.

Troubleshooting

If homemade cookies spread too much during baking, the following problems may have occurred:

- The oven temperature was too cold.
- Pure cane sugar (sucrose) was not used; fructose sugar or a blend of sugars was substituted.
- The cookie sheets were greased too heavily.
- Diet margarine or vegetable oil spreads were substituted for butter or regular stick margarine (80% fat).
- Dark brown sugar was used instead of the light brown sugar generally called for in recipes.
- The cookie sheet was still warm when the cookie dough was placed on the sheet.

If homemade cookies did not spread enough during baking, the following problems may have occurred:

- The cookie dough was over-mixed.
- The cookie dough was too cold.
- The oven temperature was too hot.
- Solid vegetable oil shortening was substituted for butter in the recipe.

If homemade cookies stick to the cookie sheet, the following problems may have occurred:

- The cookie sheets were not sufficiently cleaned between uses.
- The cookie sheets were not greased and the recipe called for greasing.
- The cookies were under-baked.
- The cookies were left on cookie sheets too long before removal.
- The cookie batter is too warm (hot kitchen).
- The cookie sheets were warm or hot before baking.

BROWNIES AND BARS

Selecting Bakeware

- Use the size of pan specified in the recipe. To check the width of a pan, measure across the top from inside edge to inside edge.

Cooling/Storing

- Cut the baked recipe into bars, squares, or other shapes when completely cool unless the recipe specifies differently. This helps prevent the bars from crumbling.
- Store bar cookies or brownies in a tightly covered container, or leave them in the pan and cover tightly with aluminum foil.

FUDGE AND CANDY

- Pick a day when the weather is cool and dry.
- Don't double, triple, or make other multiples of a fudge recipe at one time. This will affect the cooking and cooling rate, and may cause recipe failure.
- Don't substitute ingredients. Fudge and candy making are very exact, and substitutions may result in poor performance.
- Use only regular butter or margarine (80% fat) in sticks. Using diet, soft, light, or vegetable oil spread products can cause recipe failure since these products contain additional moisture or different fats.

DAZZLING
COOKIES & BITES

TOUCHED BY CHOCOLATE

secret KISSES cookies

1 cup (2 sticks) butter or margarine, softened

½ cup granulated sugar

1 teaspoon vanilla extract

1¾ cups all-purpose flour

1 cup finely chopped walnuts or almonds

36 HERSHEY'S KISSES BRAND Milk Chocolates or HERSHEY'S KISSES BRAND Milk Chocolates with Almonds

Powdered sugar

1. Beat butter, granulated sugar and vanilla with electric mixer on medium speed in large bowl until fluffy. Add flour and walnuts; beat on low speed of mixer until well blended. Cover; refrigerate 1 to 2 hours or until dough is firm enough to handle.

2. Remove wrappers from chocolates. Heat oven to 375°F. Using about 1 tablespoon dough for each cookie, shape dough around each chocolate; roll in hand to make ball. (Be sure to cover each chocolate piece completely.) Place on ungreased cookie sheet.

3. Bake 10 to 12 minutes or until cookies are set but not browned. Cool slightly; remove to wire rack. While still slightly warm, roll in powdered sugar. Cool completely. Store in tightly covered container. Roll again in powdered sugar just before serving.

VARIATION

Sift together 1 tablespoon HERSHEY'S Cocoa with ⅓ cup powdered sugar. Roll warm cookies in cocoa mixture. ■

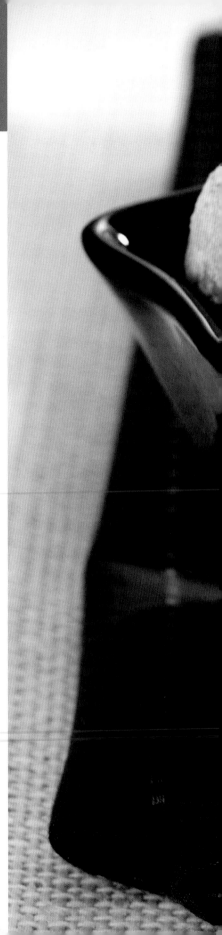

chocolate chip & toffee bits cookies

MAKES ABOUT 4 DOZEN COOKIES

2¼ cups all-purpose flour

1 teaspoon baking soda

½ teaspoon salt

¾ cup (1½ sticks) butter or margarine, softened

¾ cup granulated sugar

¾ cup packed light brown sugar

1 teaspoon vanilla extract

2 eggs

1 cup HEATH BITS 'O BRICKLE Toffee Bits

1 cup HERSHEY'S SPECIAL DARK Chocolate Chips or HERSHEY'S Semi-Sweet Chocolate Chips

1. Heat oven to 375°F.

2. Stir together flour, baking soda and salt in medium bowl. Beat butter, granulated sugar, brown sugar and vanilla in large bowl until well blended. Add eggs; beat well. Gradually add flour mixture, beating well. Stir in toffee bits and chocolate chips. Drop dough by rounded teaspoons onto ungreased cookie sheet.

3. Bake 8 to 10 minutes or until lightly browned. Cool slightly; remove from cookie sheet to wire rack. Cool completely. ■

mini brownie cups

MAKES 24 SERVINGS

¼ cup (½ stick) light margarine

2 egg whites

1 egg

¾ cup sugar

⅔ cup all-purpose flour

⅓ cup HERSHEY'S Cocoa

½ teaspoon baking powder

¼ teaspoon salt

MOCHA GLAZE
(recipe follows)

1. Heat oven to 350°F. Line small muffin cups (1¾ inches in diameter) with paper bake cups or spray with vegetable cooking spray.

2. Melt margarine in small saucepan over low heat; cool slightly. Beat egg whites and egg in small bowl with electric mixer on medium speed until foamy; gradually add sugar, beating until slightly thickened and light in color. Stir together flour, cocoa, baking powder and salt; gradually add to egg mixture, beating until blended. Gradually add melted margarine, beating just until blended. Fill muffin cups ⅔ full with batter.

3. Bake 15 to 18 minutes or until wooden pick inserted in center comes out clean. Remove from pan to wire rack. Cool completely. Prepare MOCHA GLAZE; drizzle over tops of brownie cups. Let stand until glaze is set.

MOCHA GLAZE

¼ cup powdered sugar

¾ teaspoon HERSHEY'S Cocoa

¼ teaspoon powdered instant coffee

2 teaspoons hot water

¼ teaspoon vanilla extract

Stir together powdered sugar and cocoa in small bowl. Dissolve instant coffee in water; gradually add to sugar mixture, stirring until well blended. Stir in vanilla.

double-drizzled chocolate shortbread cookies

MAKES ABOUT 6 DOZEN COOKIES

2 cups (4 sticks) butter or margarine, softened

1⅓ cups sugar

1 teaspoon vanilla extract

4 egg yolks

4 cups all-purpose flour

½ cup HERSHEY'S SPECIAL DARK Cocoa

1 teaspoon salt

1 cup chopped pecans

1 cup HERSHEY'S SPECIAL DARK Chocolate Chips or HERSHEY'S Semi-Sweet Chocolate Chips

2 tablespoons shortening (do not use butter, margarine, spread or oil), divided

1 cup REESE'S Peanut Butter Chips or HERSHEY'S Premier White Chips

1. Beat butter, sugar and vanilla until well blended. Add egg yolks, 1 at a time, beating well after each addition. Gradually add flour, cocoa and salt, beating until blended. (Batter is very stiff.)

2. Divide dough in half. Shape each part into 12-inch-long log. Roll each in pecans, pressing firmly to have pecans adhere. Wrap each roll separately in plastic wrap. Refrigerate 6 to 8 hours.

3. Heat oven to 350°F. Using a sharp knife, cut rolls into ⅜-inch slices. Place on ungreased cookie sheet. Bake 10 to 12 minutes or until set. Cool slightly. Remove from cookie sheet to wire rack. Cool completely.

4. Place chocolate chips and 1 tablespoon shortening in small microwave-safe bowl. Microwave at MEDIUM (50%) 1 minute; stir. If necessary, microwave at MEDIUM an additional 15 seconds at a time, stirring after each heating, until chips are melted and smooth when stirred. Drizzle over top of cookies. Melt peanut butter chips or white chips with remaining 1 tablespoon shortening; drizzle over chocolate. Let stand until drizzles are set. ■

MINI KISSES
milk chocolate peanut butter cookies

MAKES 18 COOKIES

¼ cup (½ stick) butter or margarine, softened

¼ cup REESE'S Creamy Peanut Butter

¼ cup granulated sugar

¼ cup packed light brown sugar

1 egg

½ teaspoon vanilla extract

⅔ cup all-purpose flour

¼ teaspoon baking soda

⅛ teaspoon salt

1¾ cups (10-ounce package) HERSHEY'S MINI KISSES BRAND Milk Chocolates

1. Heat oven to 350°F. Lightly grease cookie sheet.

2. Beat butter and peanut butter in large bowl on medium speed of electric mixer until creamy. Gradually add granulated sugar and brown sugar, beating until well mixed. Add egg and vanilla; beat until light and fluffy. Stir together flour, baking soda and salt; add to butter mixture, beating until well blended. Stir in chocolates. Drop batter by rounded tablespoons onto prepared cookie sheet.

3. Bake 10 to 12 minutes or until lightly browned. Cool slightly; remove from cookie sheet to wire rack. Cool completely. ■

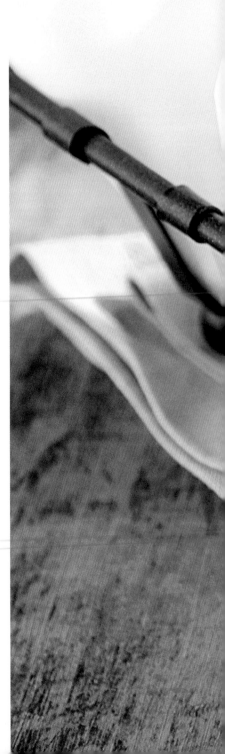

pecan MINI KISSES cups

MAKES 24 CUPS

½ cup (1 stick) butter or margarine, softened

1 package (3 ounces) cream cheese, softened

1 cup all-purpose flour

1 egg

⅔ cup packed light brown sugar

1 tablespoon butter, melted

1 teaspoon vanilla extract

Dash salt

72 (½ cup) HERSHEY'S MINI KISSES BRAND Milk Chocolates, divided

½ to ¾ cup coarsely chopped pecans

1. Beat ½ cup softened butter and cream cheese in medium bowl until blended. Add flour; beat well. Cover; refrigerate about 1 hour or until firm enough to handle.

2. Heat oven to 325°F. Stir together egg, brown sugar, 1 tablespoon melted butter, vanilla and salt in small bowl until well blended.

3. Shape chilled dough into 24 balls (1 inch each). Place balls in ungreased small muffin cups (1¾ inches in diameter). Press onto bottoms and up sides of cups. Place 2 chocolate pieces in each cup. Spoon about 1 teaspoon pecans over chocolate. Fill each cup with egg mixture.

4. Bake 25 minutes or until filling is set. Lightly press 1 chocolate into center of each cookie. Cool in pan on wire rack. ■

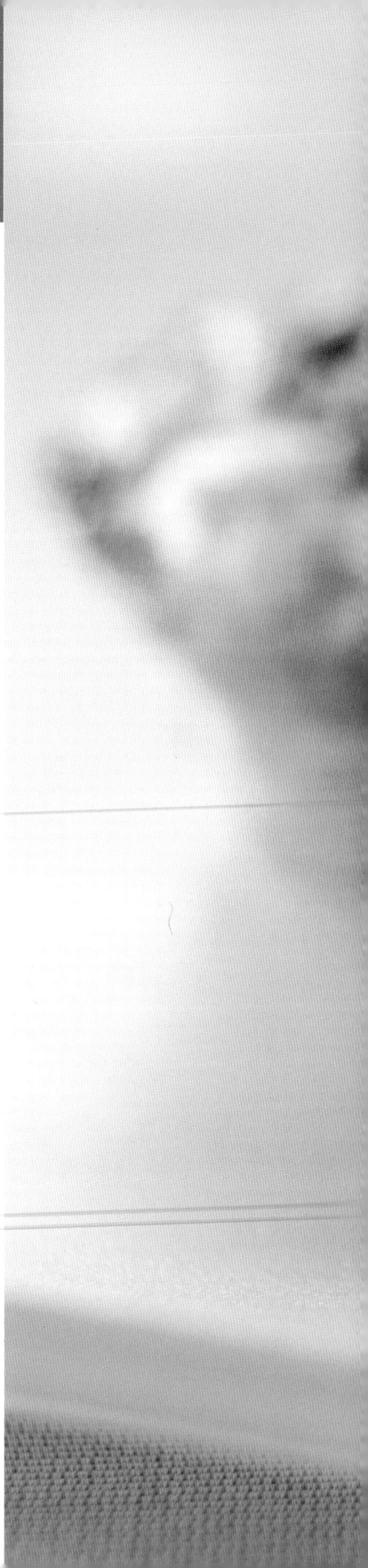

chocolate swirl lollipop cookies

MAKES ABOUT 24 COOKIES

½ cup (1 stick) butter or margarine, softened

1 cup sugar

2 eggs

1 teaspoon orange extract

1 teaspoon vanilla extract

2¼ cups all-purpose flour, divided

½ teaspoon baking soda

½ teaspoon salt

¼ teaspoon freshly grated orange peel

Few drops red and yellow food color (optional)

2 sections (½ ounce each) HERSHEY'S Unsweetened Chocolate Premium Baking Bar, melted

About 24 wooden popsicle sticks

1. Beat butter and sugar in large bowl until blended. Add eggs and extracts; beat until light and fluffy. Gradually add 1¼ cups flour, blending until smooth. Stir in remaining 1 cup flour, baking soda and salt until mixture is well blended.

2. Place half of batter in medium bowl; stir in orange peel. Stir in food color, if desired. Melt baking chocolate as directed on package; stir into remaining half of batter. Cover; refrigerate both mixtures until firm enough to roll.

3. With rolling pin or fingers, between 2 pieces of wax paper, roll chocolate and orange mixtures each into 10×8-inch rectangle. Remove wax paper; place orange mixture on top of chocolate. Starting on longest side, roll up doughs tightly, forming into 12-inch roll; wrap in plastic wrap. Refrigerate until firm.

4. Heat oven to 350°F. Remove plastic wrap from roll; cut into ½-inch-wide slices. Place on cookie sheet at least 3 inches apart. Insert popsicle stick into each cookie.

5. Bake 8 to 10 minutes or until cookie is almost set. Cool slightly; remove from cookie sheet to wire rack. Cool completely. Decorate and tie with ribbon, if desired. ■

double chocolate coconut oatmeal cookies

MAKES ABOUT 2½ DOZEN COOKIES

1 cup shortening

1¾ cups packed light brown sugar

3 eggs

2 teaspoons vanilla extract

1⅓ cups all-purpose flour

½ cup HERSHEY'S Cocoa

2 teaspoons baking soda

¼ teaspoon salt

½ cup water

3 cups rolled oats or quick-cooking oats

2 cups (12-ounce package) HERSHEY'S SPECIAL DARK Chocolate Chips or HERSHEY'S Semi-Sweet Chocolate Chips, divided

2 cups MOUNDS Sweetened Coconut Flakes, divided

1 cup coarsely chopped nuts

Purchase the freshest nuts you can find for baking—they should be sweet when tasted.

1. Beat shortening, brown sugar, eggs and vanilla in large bowl until well blended. Stir together flour, cocoa, baking soda and salt; add alternately with water to shortening mixture. Stir in oats, 1 cup chocolate chips, 1 cup coconut and nuts, blending well. Cover; refrigerate 2 hours.

2. Heat oven to 350°F. Lightly grease cookie sheet or line with parchment paper. Using ¼-cup ice cream scoop or measuring cup, drop dough about 4 inches apart onto prepared cookie sheet. Sprinkle cookie tops with remaining coconut. Top with remaining chocolate chips (about 9 chips per cookie); lightly press into dough.

3. Bake 10 to 12 minutes or until set (do not overbake). Cool slightly; remove from cookie sheet to wire rack. Cool completely. ■

KISSES macaroon cookies

MAKES ABOUT 4 DOZEN COOKIES

⅓ cup butter or margarine, softened

1 package (3 ounces) cream cheese, softened

¾ cup sugar

1 egg yolk

2 teaspoons almond extract

2 teaspoons orange juice

1¼ cups all-purpose flour

2 teaspoons baking powder

¼ teaspoon salt

5 cups MOUNDS Sweetened Coconut Flakes, divided

48 HERSHEY'S KISSES BRAND Milk Chocolates

1. Beat butter, cream cheese and sugar with electric mixer on medium speed in large bowl until well blended. Add egg yolk, almond extract and orange juice; beat well. Stir together flour, baking powder and salt; gradually add to butter mixture. Stir in 3 cups coconut. Cover; refrigerate 1 hour or until firm enough to handle. Meanwhile, remove wrappers from chocolates.

2. Heat oven to 350°F.

3. Shape dough into 1-inch balls; roll in remaining 2 cups coconut. Place on ungreased cookie sheet.

4. Bake 10 to 12 minutes or until lightly browned. Immediately press chocolate piece into center of each cookie. Cool 1 minute. Carefully remove to wire rack and cool completely. ■

peanut butter cut-out cookies

½ cup (1 stick) butter or margarine

1 cup REESE'S Peanut Butter Chips

⅔ cup packed light brown sugar

1 egg

¾ teaspoon vanilla extract

1⅓ cups all-purpose flour

¾ teaspoon baking soda

½ cup finely chopped pecans

CHOCOLATE CHIP GLAZE
(recipe follows)

1. Place butter and peanut butter chips in medium saucepan; cook over low heat, stirring constantly, until melted. Pour into large bowl; add brown sugar, egg and vanilla, beating until well blended. Stir in flour, baking soda and pecans, blending well. Refrigerate 15 to 20 minutes or until firm enough to roll.

2. Heat oven to 350°F.

3. Roll a small portion of dough at a time on lightly floured board, or between 2 pieces of wax paper, to ¼-inch thickness. (Keep remaining dough in refrigerator.) With cookie cutters, cut dough into desired shapes; place on ungreased cookie sheets.

4. Bake 7 to 8 minutes or until almost set (do not overbake). Cool 1 minute; remove from cookie sheets to wire racks. Cool completely. Drizzle CHOCOLATE CHIP GLAZE onto each cookie; allow to set.

CHOCOLATE CHIP GLAZE

Place 1 cup HERSHEY'S SPECIAL DARK Chocolate Chips or HERSHEY'S Semi-Sweet Chocolate Chips and 1 tablespoon shortening (do not use butter, margarine spread or oil) in small microwave-safe bowl. Microwave at MEDIUM (50%) 1 minute; stir. If necessary, microwave at MEDIUM an additional 15 seconds at a time, stirring after each heating, just until chips are melted and mixture is smooth. ■

peanut butter blossoms

MAKES ABOUT 4 DOZEN COOKIES

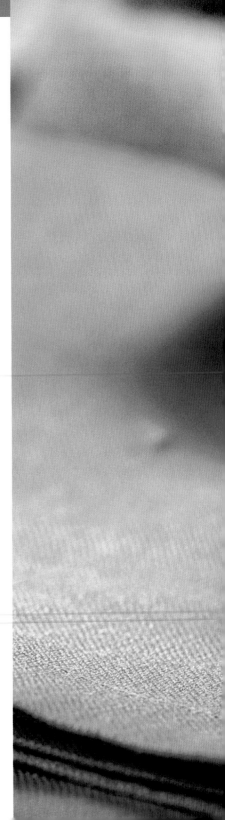

48 HERSHEY'S KISSES BRAND Milk Chocolates

¾ cup REESE'S Creamy Peanut Butter

½ cup shortening

⅓ cup granulated sugar

⅓ cup packed light brown sugar

1 egg

2 tablespoons milk

1 teaspoon vanilla extract

1½ cups all-purpose flour

1 teaspoon baking soda

½ teaspoon salt

Granulated sugar

1. Heat oven to 375°F. Remove wrappers from chocolates.

2. Beat peanut butter and shortening with electric mixer on medium speed in large bowl until well blended. Add ⅓ cup granulated sugar and brown sugar; beat until fluffy. Add egg, milk and vanilla; beat well. Stir together flour, baking soda and salt; gradually beat into peanut butter mixture.

3. Shape dough into 1-inch balls. Roll in additional granulated sugar; place on ungreased cookie sheet.

4. Bake 8 to 10 minutes or until lightly browned. Immediately press a chocolate into center of each cookie; cookies will crack around edges. Remove to wire racks and cool completely. ■

rich cocoa crinkle cookies

MAKES ABOUT 6 DOZEN COOKIES

2 cups granulated sugar

¾ cup vegetable oil

1 cup HERSHEY'S Cocoa

4 eggs

2 teaspoons vanilla extract

2⅓ cups all-purpose flour

2 teaspoons baking powder

½ teaspoon salt

Powdered sugar

1. Combine granulated sugar and oil in large bowl; add cocoa, beating until well blended. Beat in eggs and vanilla. Stir together flour, baking powder and salt. Gradually add to cocoa mixture, beating well.

2. Cover; refrigerate until dough is firm enough to handle, at least 6 hours.

3. Heat oven to 350°F. Grease cookie sheet or line with parchment paper. Shape dough into 1-inch balls; roll in powdered sugar to coat. Place about 2 inches apart on prepared cookie sheet.

4. Bake 10 to 12 minutes or until almost no indentation remains when touched lightly and tops are crackled. Cool slightly. Remove from cookie sheet to wire rack. Cool completely. ■

almond shortbread cookies with chocolate filling

MAKES ABOUT 44 SANDWICH COOKIES

¾ cup sliced almonds, toasted*

1 cup (2 sticks) butter or margarine, softened

¾ cup sugar

3 egg yolks

¾ teaspoon almond extract

2 cups all-purpose flour

CHOCOLATE FILLING (recipe follows)

Powdered sugar (optional)

*To toast almonds: Heat oven to 350°F. Spread almonds in thin layer in shallow baking pan. Bake 8 to 10 minutes, stirring occasionally, until light golden brown; cool.

1. Finely chop almonds; set aside.

2. Beat butter and sugar in large bowl until creamy. Add egg yolks and almond extract; beat well. Gradually add flour, beating until well blended. Stir in almonds. Refrigerate dough 1 to 2 hours or until firm enough to handle.

3. Heat oven to 350°F. On well-floured surface, roll about one-fourth of dough to about ⅛-inch thickness (keep remaining dough in refrigerator). Using 2-inch round cookie cutter, cut into equal number of rounds. Place on ungreased cookie sheet. Repeat with remaining dough.

4. Bake 8 to 10 minutes or until almost set. Cool slightly; remove from cookie sheet to wire rack. Cool completely. Spread about one measuring teaspoonful CHOCOLATE FILLING onto bottom of one cookie. Top with second cookie; gently press together. Repeat with remaining cookies. Allow to set, about 1 hour. Lightly sift powdered sugar over top of cookies, if desired. Cover; store at room temperature.

CHOCOLATE FILLING

Combine 1 cup HERSHEY'S Milk Chocolate Chips** and ⅓ cup whipping cream in small saucepan. Stir constantly over low heat until mixture is smooth. Remove from heat. Cool about 20 minutes or until slightly thickened and spreadable.

**HERSHEY'S SPECIAL DARK Chocolate Chips or HERSHEY'S Semi-Sweet Chocolate Chips may also be used. ■

HERSHEY'S double chocolate MINI KISSES cookies

MAKES ABOUT 3½ DOZEN COOKIES

1 cup (2 sticks) butter or margarine, softened

1½ cups sugar

2 eggs

2 teaspoons vanilla extract

2 cups all-purpose flour

⅔ cup HERSHEY'S Cocoa

¾ teaspoon baking soda

¼ teaspoon salt

1¾ cups (10-ounce package) HERSHEY'S MINI KISSES BRAND Milk Chocolates

½ cup coarsely chopped nuts (optional)

1. Heat oven to 350°F.

2. Beat butter, sugar, eggs and vanilla with electric mixer on medium speed in large bowl until light and fluffy. Stir together flour, cocoa, baking soda and salt; add to butter mixture, beating until well blended. Stir in chocolates and nuts, if desired. Drop by tablespoons onto ungreased cookie sheet.

3. Bake 8 to 10 minutes or just until set. Cool slightly. Remove to wire rack and cool completely. ■

BOUNTIFUL
BROWNIES & BARS

INDULGE IN PERFECTION

chocolate fudge pecan pie bars

MAKES ABOUT 3 DOZEN BARS

2⅔ cups all-purpose flour

1¼ cups packed light brown sugar, divided

1 cup (2 sticks) cold butter or margarine

4 eggs

1 cup light corn syrup

1 package (4 ounces) HERSHEY'S Unsweetened Chocolate Premium Baking Bar, unwrapped and melted

2 teaspoons vanilla extract

½ teaspoon salt

2 cups coarsely chopped pecans

1. Heat oven to 350°F. Grease 15½×10½× 1-inch jelly-roll pan.

2. Stir together flour and ¼ cup brown sugar in large bowl. With pastry blender, cut in butter until mixture resembles coarse crumbs; press onto bottom of prepared pan.

3. Bake 10 to 15 minutes or until set. Remove from oven. With back of spoon, lightly press crust into corners and against sides of pan.

4. Beat eggs, corn syrup, remaining 1 cup brown sugar, melted chocolate, vanilla and salt; stir in pecans. Pour mixture evenly over warm crust. Return to oven.

5. Bake 25 to 30 minutes or until chocolate filling is set. Cool completely in pan on wire rack. Cut into bars. ■

chocolate almond macaroon bars

MAKES ABOUT 36 BARS

2 cups chocolate wafer cookie crumbs

6 tablespoons butter or margarine, melted

6 tablespoons powdered sugar

1 can (14 ounces) sweetened condensed milk (not evaporated milk)

3¾ cups MOUNDS Sweetened Coconut Flakes

1 cup almond slices, toasted* (optional)

1 cup HERSHEY'S SPECIAL DARK Chocolate Chips or HERSHEY'S Semi-Sweet Chocolate Chips

¼ cup whipping cream

½ cup HERSHEY'S Premier White Chips

*To toast almonds: Heat oven to 350°F. Spread almonds evenly on shallow baking sheet. Bake 5 to 8 minutes or until lightly browned.

1. Heat oven to 350°F. Grease 13×9×2-inch baking pan.

2. Combine crumbs, melted butter and sugar in large bowl. Firmly press crumb mixture on bottom of prepared pan. Stir together sweetened condensed milk, coconut and almonds, if desired, in large bowl, mixing well. Carefully drop mixture by spoonfuls over crust; spread evenly.

3. Bake 20 to 25 minutes or until coconut edges just begin to brown. Cool.

4. Place chocolate chips and whipping cream in medium microwave-safe bowl. Microwave at MEDIUM (50%) 1 minute; stir. If necessary, microwave at MEDIUM an additional 15 seconds at a time, stirring after each heating, until chips are melted and mixture is smooth when stirred. Cool until slightly thickened; spread over cooled bars. Sprinkle top with white chips. Cover; refrigerate several hours or until thoroughly chilled. Cut into bars. Refrigerate leftovers. ■

peanut butter glazed chocolate bars

MAKES ABOUT 40 BARS

¾ cup (1½ sticks) butter or margarine

½ cup HERSHEY'S Cocoa

1½ cups sugar

1½ teaspoons vanilla extract

3 eggs

1¼ cups all-purpose flour

¼ teaspoon baking powder

PEANUT BUTTER FILLING AND GLAZE (recipe follows)

CHOCOLATE DRIZZLE (recipe follows)

1. Heat oven to 350°F. Line 15½×10½× 1-inch jelly-roll pan with foil; grease foil.

2. Melt butter in medium saucepan over low heat. Add cocoa; stir constantly until smooth. Remove from heat; stir in sugar and vanilla. Beat in eggs, one at a time, until well combined. Stir in flour and baking powder. Spread batter evenly in prepared pan.

3. Bake 14 to 16 minutes or until top springs back when touched lightly in center. Remove from oven; cool 2 minutes. Invert onto wire rack. Peel off foil; turn right side up on wire rack to cool completely.

4. Prepare PEANUT BUTTER FILLING AND GLAZE. Cut brownie in half; spread half of glaze evenly on one half. Top with second half; spread with remaining glaze. Cool until glaze is set. Prepare CHOCOLATE DRIZZLE; drizzle over glaze. After chocolate is set, cut into bars.

PEANUT BUTTER FILLING AND GLAZE

Combine ⅓ cup sugar and ⅓ cup water in small saucepan; cook over medium heat to boiling. Remove from heat; immediately add 1⅔ cups (10-ounce package) REESE'S Peanut Butter Chips. Stir until melted. Cool slightly.

MAKES ABOUT 1⅓ CUPS GLAZE

CHOCOLATE DRIZZLE

Place ⅓ cup HERSHEY'S SPECIAL DARK Chocolate Chips or HERSHEY'S Semi-Sweet Chocolate Chips and 1 teaspoon shortening (do not use butter, margarine, spread or oil) in small microwave-safe bowl. Microwave at MEDIUM (50%) 30 seconds to 1 minute or until chips are melted and mixture is smooth when stirred. ■

peanut butter fudge brownie bars

MAKES 36 BARS

1 cup (2 sticks) butter or margarine, melted

1½ cups sugar

2 eggs

1 teaspoon vanilla extract

1¼ cups all-purpose flour

⅔ cup HERSHEY'S Cocoa

¼ cup milk

1¼ cups chopped pecans or walnuts, divided

½ cup (1 stick) butter or margarine

1⅔ cups (10-ounce package) REESE'S Peanut Butter Chips

1 can (14 ounces) sweetened condensed milk (not evaporated milk)

¼ cup HERSHEY'S SPECIAL DARK Chocolate Chips or HERSHEY'S Semi-Sweet Chocolate Chips

1. Heat oven to 350°F. Grease 13×9× 2-inch baking pan.

2. Beat melted butter, sugar, eggs and vanilla in large bowl with electric mixer on medium speed until well blended. Add flour, cocoa and milk; beat until blended. Stir in 1 cup nuts. Spread in prepared pan.

3. Bake 25 to 30 minutes or just until edges begin to pull away from sides of pan. Cool completely in pan on wire rack.

4. Melt ½ cup butter and peanut butter chips in medium saucepan over low heat, stirring constantly. Add sweetened condensed milk, stirring until smooth; pour over baked layer.

5. Place chocolate chips in small microwave-safe bowl. Microwave at MEDIUM (50%) 45 seconds or just until chips are melted when stirred. Drizzle bars with melted chocolate; sprinkle with remaining ¼ cup nuts. Refrigerate 1 hour or until firm. Cut into bars. Cover; refrigerate leftover bars. ■

MINI KISSES fruit bars

MAKES 36 BARS

1½ cups all-purpose flour

1½ cups quick-cooking rolled oats

1 cup packed light brown sugar

1 teaspoon baking powder

¾ cup (1½ sticks) butter or margarine, softened

1 jar (10 to 12 ounces) raspberry jam

1¾ cups (10-ounce package) HERSHEY'S MINI KISSES BRAND Milk Chocolates

½ cup chopped nuts (optional)

1. Heat oven to 350°F. Lightly grease 13×9×2-inch baking pan.

2. Combine flour, oats, brown sugar and baking powder in large bowl. Cut butter into flour mixture with pastry blender or two knives until crumbly. Remove 2 cups crumb mixture; set aside.

3. Press remaining crumb mixture onto bottom of prepared pan. Stir jam to soften; carefully spread over crumb mixture. Sprinkle chocolates evenly over jam. Cover with reserved crumbs. Sprinkle nuts over top, if desired; press firmly.

4. Bake 40 to 45 minutes or until lightly browned. Cool completely in pan on wire rack. Cut into bars. ■

chewy toffee almond bars

MAKES ABOUT 36 BARS

1 cup (2 sticks) butter, softened

½ cup sugar

2 cups all-purpose flour

1⅓ cups (8-ounce package) HEATH BITS 'O BRICKLE Toffee Bits

¾ cup light corn syrup

1 cup sliced almonds, divided

¾ cup MOUNDS Sweetened Coconut Flakes, divided

Jazz up your baked desserts, custards, puddings, pies and fruit-based desserts with coconut—great for both baking and decorating.

1. Heat oven to 350°F. Grease sides of 13×9×2-inch baking pan.

2. Beat butter and sugar until fluffy. Gradually add flour, beating until well blended. Press dough evenly in prepared pan.

3. Bake 15 to 20 minutes or until edges are lightly browned. Meanwhile, combine toffee bits and corn syrup in medium saucepan. Cook over medium heat, stirring constantly, until toffee is melted (about 10 to 12 minutes). Stir in ½ cup almonds and ½ cup coconut. Spread toffee mixture to within ¼-inch of edges of crust. Sprinkle remaining ½ cup almonds and remaining ¼ cup coconut over top.

4. Bake an additional 15 minutes or until bubbly. Cool completely in pan on wire rack. Cut into bars. ■

five layer bars

¾ cup (1½ sticks) butter or margarine

1¾ cups graham cracker crumbs

¼ cup HERSHEY'S Cocoa

2 tablespoons sugar

1 can (14 ounces) sweetened condensed milk (not evaporated milk)

1 cup HERSHEY'S SPECIAL DARK Chocolate Chips or HERSHEY'S Semi-Sweet Chocolate Chips

1 cup raisins, chopped dried apricots or miniature marshmallows

1 cup chopped nuts

1. Heat oven to 350°F. Place butter in 13×9×2-inch baking pan. Heat in oven until melted; remove pan from oven.

2. Stir together crumbs, cocoa and sugar; sprinkle evenly over butter. Pour sweetened condensed milk evenly over crumb mixture. Sprinkle with chocolate chips and raisins. Sprinkle nuts on top; press down firmly.

3. Bake 25 to 30 minutes or until lightly browned. Cool completely in pan on wire rack. Cover with foil; let stand at room temperature 6 to 8 hours. Cut into bars.

GOLDEN BARS

Substitute 1 cup REESE'S Peanut Butter Chips for chocolate chips. Sprinkle 1 cup golden raisins or chopped dried apricots over chips. Proceed as above. ■

chocolate orange cheesecake bars

MAKES 24 BARS

CRUST

1 cup all-purpose flour

½ cup packed light brown sugar

¼ teaspoon ground cinnamon (optional)

⅓ cup shortening

½ cup chopped pecans

CHOCOLATE ORANGE FILLING

1 package (8 ounces) cream cheese, softened

⅔ cup granulated sugar

⅓ cup HERSHEY'S Cocoa

¼ cup milk

1 egg

1 teaspoon vanilla extract

¼ teaspoon freshly grated orange peel

Pecan halves (optional)

1. Heat oven to 350°F.

2. For CRUST, stir together flour, brown sugar and cinnamon, if desired, in large bowl. Cut shortening into flour mixture with pastry blender or two knives until mixture resembles coarse crumbs. Stir in chopped pecans. Reserve ¾ cup flour mixture. Press remaining mixture firmly onto bottom of ungreased 9-inch square baking pan. Bake 10 minutes or until lightly browned.

3. For CHOCOLATE ORANGE FILLING, beat cream cheese and sugar with electric mixer on medium speed in medium bowl until fluffy. Add cocoa, milk, egg, vanilla and orange peel; beat until smooth.

4. Spread filling over warm crust. Sprinkle with reserved flour mixture. Press pecan halves lightly onto top, if desired. Return to oven. Bake 25 to 30 minutes or until lightly browned. Cool; cut into bars. Cover; refrigerate leftover bars. ∎

best fudgey pecan brownies

MAKES ABOUT 16 BROWNIES

½ cup (1 stick) butter or margarine, melted

1 cup sugar

1 teaspoon vanilla extract

2 eggs

½ cup all-purpose flour

⅓ cup HERSHEY'S Cocoa

¼ teaspoon baking powder

¼ teaspoon salt

½ cup coarsely chopped pecans

CHOCOLATE PECAN FROSTING (recipe follows)

Pecan halves

1. Heat oven to 350°F. Lightly grease 8- or 9-inch square baking pan.

2. Beat butter, sugar and vanilla with spoon in large bowl. Add eggs; beat well. Stir together flour, cocoa, baking powder and salt; gradually add to egg mixture, beating until well blended. Stir in chopped pecans. Spread in prepared pan.

3. Bake 20 to 25 minutes or until brownies begin to pull away from sides of pan. Meanwhile, prepare CHOCOLATE PECAN FROSTING. Spread warm frosting over warm brownies. Garnish with pecan halves. Cool completely; cut into squares.

CHOCOLATE PECAN FROSTING

1⅓ cups powdered sugar

2 tablespoons HERSHEY'S Cocoa

3 tablespoons butter or margarine

2 tablespoons milk

¼ teaspoon vanilla extract

¼ cup chopped pecans

1. Place powdered sugar and cocoa in medium bowl.

2. Heat butter and milk in small saucepan over low heat until butter is melted. Gradually beat into cocoa mixture, beating until smooth. Stir in vanilla and pecans.

MAKES ABOUT 1 CUP FROSTING ■

chocolate seven layer bars

MAKES 36 BARS

1½ cups finely crushed thin pretzels or pretzel sticks

¾ cup (1½ sticks) butter or margarine, melted

1 can (14 ounces) sweetened condensed milk (not evaporated milk)

1 package (4 ounces) HERSHEY'S Unsweetened Chocolate Premium Baking Bar, broken into pieces

2 cups miniature marshmallows

1 cup MOUNDS Sweetened Coconut Flakes

1 cup coarsely chopped pecans

1 package (4 ounces) HERSHEY'S SPECIAL DARK Chocolate Premium Baking Bar, broken into pieces

1 tablespoon shortening (do not use butter, margarine, spread or oil)

1. Heat oven to 350°F. Combine pretzels and melted butter in small bowl; press evenly onto bottom of ungreased 13× 9×2-inch baking pan.

2. Place sweetened condensed milk and unsweetened chocolate in small microwave-safe bowl. Microwave at MEDIUM (50%) 1 minute; stir. If necessary, microwave at MEDIUM an additional 15 seconds at a time, stirring after each heating, until mixture is melted and smooth when stirred. Carefully pour over pretzel layer in pan. Top with marshmallows, coconut and pecans; press firmly down onto chocolate layer.

3. Bake 25 to 30 minutes or until lightly browned; cool completely in pan on wire rack.

4. Melt SPECIAL DARK chocolate and shortening in small microwave-safe bowl at MEDIUM (50%) 1 minute or until melted when stirred; drizzle over entire top. Cut into bars. Refrigerate 15 minutes or until glaze is set. ■

chunky macadamia bars

MAKES 24 BARS

¾ cup (1½ sticks) butter or margarine, softened

1 cup packed light brown sugar

½ cup granulated sugar

1 egg

1 teaspoon vanilla extract

2¼ cups all-purpose flour

1 teaspoon baking soda

1¾ cups (10-ounce package) HERSHEY'S MINI KISSES BRAND Milk Chocolates, divided

¾ cup MAUNA LOA Macadamia Baking Pieces

VANILLA GLAZE (recipe follows)

1. Heat oven to 375°F.

2. Beat butter, brown sugar and granulated sugar in large bowl until fluffy. Add egg and vanilla; beat well. Add flour and baking soda; blend well. Stir in 1 cup chocolate pieces and nuts; press into ungreased 13×9×2-inch baking pan. Sprinkle with remaining ¾ cup chocolates.

3. Bake 22 to 25 minutes or until golden brown. Cool completely in pan on wire rack. Drizzle VANILLA GLAZE over top; allow to set. Cut into bars.

VANILLA GLAZE

Combine 1 cup powdered sugar, 2 tablespoons milk and ½ teaspoon vanilla extract in small bowl; stir until smooth.

MAKES ⅓ CUP GLAZE ■

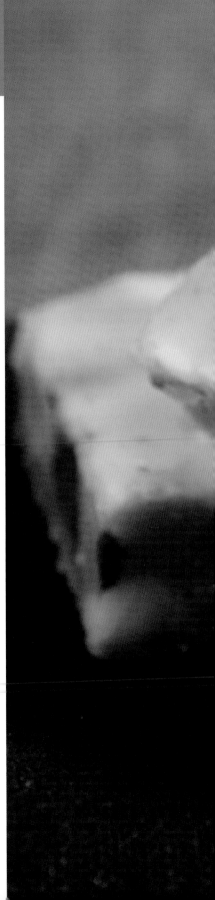

cranberry orange ricotta cheese brownies

MAKES ABOUT 16 BROWNIES

½ cup (1 stick) butter or margarine, melted

¾ cup sugar

1 teaspoon vanilla extract

2 eggs

¾ cup all-purpose flour

½ cup HERSHEY'S Cocoa

½ teaspoon baking powder

½ teaspoon salt

CHEESE FILLING (recipe follows)

1. Heat oven to 350°F. Grease 9-inch square baking pan.

2. Stir together butter, sugar and vanilla in medium bowl; add eggs, beating well. Stir together flour, cocoa, baking powder and salt; add to butter mixture, mixing thoroughly. Spread half of chocolate batter in prepared pan. Spread CHEESE FILLING over top. Drop remaining chocolate batter by teaspoonfuls onto CHEESE FILLING.

3. Bake 40 to 45 minutes or until wooden pick inserted in center comes out clean. Cool completely in pan on wire rack. Cut into squares. Refrigerate leftover brownies.

CHEESE FILLING

1 cup ricotta cheese

¼ cup sugar

3 tablespoons whole-berry cranberry sauce

2 tablespoons cornstarch

1 egg

¼ to ½ teaspoon freshly grated orange peel

4 drops red food color (optional)

Beat ricotta cheese, sugar, cranberry sauce, cornstarch and egg in small bowl until smooth. Stir in orange peel and food color, if desired. ■

chocolate streusel bars

MAKES ABOUT 36 BARS

1¾ cups all-purpose flour

1 cup sugar

¼ cup HERSHEY'S Cocoa

½ cup (1 stick) butter or margarine

1 egg

1 can (14 ounces) sweetened
condensed milk
(not evaporated milk)

2 cups (12-ounce package)
HERSHEY'S SPECIAL DARK Chocolate
Chips or HERSHEY'S Semi-Sweet
Chocolate Chips, divided

1 cup coarsely chopped nuts

1. Heat oven to 350°F. Grease 13×9×2-inch baking pan.

2. Stir together flour, sugar and cocoa in large bowl. Cut in butter until mixture resembles coarse crumbs. Add egg; mix well. Set aside 1½ cups mixture. Press remaining mixture onto bottom of prepared pan.

3. Bake 10 minutes. Meanwhile, place sweetened condensed milk and 1 cup chocolate chips in medium microwave-safe bowl; stir. Microwave at MEDIUM (50%) 1 to 1½ minutes or until chips are melted and mixture is smooth when stirred; pour over crust. Add nuts and remaining chips to reserved crumb mixture. Sprinkle over top.

4. Bake an additional 25 to 30 minutes or until center is almost set. Cool completely in pan on wire rack. Cut into bars. ■

english toffee bars

MAKES ABOUT 36 BARS

2 cups all-purpose flour

1 cup packed light brown sugar

½ cup (1 stick) cold butter

1 cup pecan halves

TOFFEE TOPPING
(recipe follows)

1 cup HERSHEY'S Milk
Chocolate Chips

1. Heat oven to 350°F.

2. Combine flour and brown sugar in large bowl. With pastry blender or fork, cut in butter until fine crumbs form (a few large crumbs may remain). Press mixture onto bottom of ungreased 13×9×2-inch baking pan. Sprinkle pecans over crust. Prepare TOFFEE TOPPING; drizzle evenly over pecans and crust.

3. Bake 20 to 22 minutes or until topping is bubbly and golden; remove from oven. Immediately sprinkle milk chocolate chips evenly over top; press gently onto surface. Cool completely in pan on wire rack. Cut into bars.

TOFFEE TOPPING

Combine ⅔ cup butter and ⅓ cup packed light brown sugar in small saucepan; cook over medium heat, stirring constantly, until mixture comes to a boil. Continue boiling, stirring constantly, 30 seconds. Use immediately. ■

CLASSIC

CAKES

CREATE A UNIQUE EXPERIENCE

collector's cocoa cake

MAKES 8 TO 10 SERVINGS

¾ cup (1½ sticks) butter or margarine, softened

1¾ cups sugar

2 eggs

1 teaspoon vanilla extract

2 cups all-purpose flour

¾ cup HERSHEY'S Cocoa or HERSHEY'S SPECIAL DARK Cocoa

1¼ teaspoons baking soda

½ teaspoon salt

1⅓ cups water

ONE-BOWL BUTTERCREAM FROSTING or FLUFFY PEANUT BUTTER FROSTING (recipes follow)

1. Heat oven to 350°F. Grease and flour two 8- or 9-inch round baking pans.

2. Beat butter and sugar in large bowl until fluffy. Add eggs and vanilla; beat 1 minute on medium speed of mixer. Stir together flour, cocoa, baking soda and salt; add alternately with water to butter mixture, beating until well blended. Pour batter into prepared pans.

3. Bake 35 to 40 minutes for 8-inch layers; 30 to 35 minutes for 9-inch layers or until wooden pick inserted in centers comes out clean. Cool 10 minutes; remove from pans to wire racks. Cool completely.

4. Frost with ONE-BOWL BUTTERCREAM FROSTING or FLUFFY PEANUT BUTTER FROSTING.

ONE-BOWL BUTTERCREAM FROSTING

6 tablespoons butter or margarine, softened

2⅔ cups powdered sugar

½ cup HERSHEY'S Cocoa or HERSHEY'S SPECIAL DARK Cocoa

⅓ cup milk

1 teaspoon vanilla extract

Beat butter in medium bowl. Add powdered sugar and cocoa alternately with milk; beat to spreading consistency (additional milk may be needed). Stir in vanilla.

MAKES ABOUT 2 CUPS FROSTING

FLUFFY PEANUT BUTTER FROSTING

1 cup milk

3 tablespoons all-purpose flour

1 cup sugar

½ cup REESE'S Creamy Peanut Butter

½ cup shortening

1 teaspoon vanilla extract

Dash salt

1. Gradually stir milk into flour in small saucepan. Cook over low heat, stirring constantly, until very thick. Transfer to medium bowl; press plastic wrap directly on surface. Cool to room temperature, about ½ hour.

2. Add sugar, peanut butter, shortening, vanilla and salt. Beat on high speed of mixer until frosting becomes fluffy and sugar is completely dissolved.

MAKES ABOUT 3 CUPS FROSTING ■

chocolate cherry delight cake

MAKES 12 SERVINGS

1 cup sugar

1 cup all-purpose flour

⅓ cup HERSHEY'S Cocoa

¾ teaspoon baking soda

¾ teaspoon baking powder

Dash salt

½ cup nonfat milk

¼ cup frozen egg substitute, thawed

¼ cup vegetable oil

1 teaspoon vanilla extract

½ cup boiling water

WHIPPED TOPPING (recipe follows)

1 can (20 ounces) lower calorie cherry pie filling, chilled

1. Heat oven to 350°F. Line bottom of two 9-inch round pans with wax paper.

2. Combine sugar, flour, cocoa, baking soda, baking powder and salt in large bowl. Add milk, egg substitute, oil and vanilla; beat on medium speed of mixer 2 minutes. Stir in boiling water. (Batter will be thin.) Pour into prepared pans.

3. Bake 18 to 22 minutes or until wooden pick inserted in centers comes out clean. Cool 10 minutes; remove from pans to wire racks. Carefully remove wax paper. Cool completely.

4. To assemble dessert, place one cake layer on serving plate. Spread with half of WHIPPED TOPPING; top with half of pie filling. Top with second cake layer. Spread with remaining topping and pie filling. Refrigerate at least one hour.

WHIPPED TOPPING

Blend ½ cup cold nonfat milk, ½ teaspoon vanilla extract and 1 envelope (1.3 ounces) dry whipped topping mix in small, deep narrow-bottom bowl. Whip at high speed with mixer until topping peaks, about 2 minutes. Continue beating 2 minutes longer until topping is light and fluffy. ■

mocha molten chocolate cake

MAKES 4 INDIVIDUAL (6-OUNCE) CAKES

FROZEN CHOCOLATE
(recipe follows)

2 teaspoons instant coffee granules

¼ cup water

1 cup all-purpose flour

½ cup plus 1 tablespoon HERSHEY'S Cocoa

⅛ teaspoon salt

¾ cup (1½ sticks) plus 2 tablespoons butter, softened

1¼ cups sugar, divided

2 teaspoons vanilla extract

3 eggs

MOCHA CREAM
(recipe follows)

1. Prepare FROZEN CHOCOLATE.

2. Heat oven to 425°F. Butter sides and bottom of four 6-ounce ramekins. Place on baking sheet.

3. Dissolve coffee granules in water; set aside. Stir together flour, cocoa and salt; set aside.

4. Beat butter in large bowl with electric mixer until light and fluffy. Set aside 1 tablespoon sugar; gradually beat in remaining sugar, vanilla and dissolved coffee, beating thoroughly.

5. Separate egg yolks from the egg whites. One at a time, add egg yolks to butter mixture, beating well after each addition.

6. In separate bowl, beat egg whites at low speed until frothy. Gradually increasing to high speed, beat the whites until soft peaks start to form. Add remaining tablespoon sugar, one teaspoon at a time, beating until stiff, shiny peaks form.

7. Fold one-third of the cocoa mixture and one-third of the egg whites into the butter mixture. One-half at a time, gently fold remaining cocoa mixture and egg whites into mixture.

8. Spoon about ⅔ cup batter into each ramekin. Place heaping teaspoon FROZEN CHOCOLATE mixture on center of each batter-filled ramekin. Spoon about ¼ cup of remaining batter over FROZEN CHOCOLATE making sure to cover completely.

9. Bake 15 to 20 minutes or until tops have started to crack.

10. While cakes are baking, reheat remaining FROZEN CHOCOLATE and make MOCHA CREAM.

11. To serve, carefully invert cake onto large dinner plate. Spoon MOCHA CREAM around base of cake; dust with powdered sugar. Garnish as desired. Serve immediately with the warmed chocolate sauce.

FROZEN CHOCOLATE

1 cup HERSHEY'S SPECIAL DARK Chocolate Chips

1 teaspoon powdered instant coffee

¾ cup heavy cream

2 tablespoons light corn syrup

1 teaspoon vanilla extract

Place chocolate chips and instant coffee in medium mixing bowl. Stir together cream and corn syrup in medium saucepan. Cook over medium heat, stirring constantly with wooden spoon until mixture comes to a boil. Pour hot cream over chocolate, let stand 30 seconds; stir until chocolate is melted and mixture is smooth. Stir in vanilla. Pour chocolate mixture into shallow bowl or dish. Cool slightly. Freeze at least 3 to 4 hours (mixture will not freeze completely).

MOCHA CREAM

1 cup (½ pint) whipping cream

3 tablespoons powdered sugar

1 tablespoon HERSHEY'S Cocoa

2 teaspoons instant coffee granules

1 teaspoon vanilla extract

Beat cream, powdered sugar, cocoa, coffee granules and vanilla in small mixer bowl until cream starts to thicken, but is still pourable. Do not overbeat. ∎

chocolate cake fingers

1 cup sugar

1 cup all-purpose flour

⅓ cup HERSHEY'S Cocoa

¾ teaspoon baking powder

¾ teaspoon baking soda

½ cup nonfat milk

¼ cup frozen egg substitute, thawed

¼ cup canola oil or vegetable oil

1 teaspoon vanilla extract

½ cup boiling water

Powdered sugar

1 teaspoon freshly grated orange peel

1½ cups frozen light non-dairy whipped topping, thawed

1. Heat oven to 350°F. Line bottom of 13×9×2-inch baking pan with wax paper.

2. Stir together sugar, flour, cocoa, baking powder and baking soda in large bowl. Add milk, egg substitute, oil and vanilla; beat on medium speed of mixer 2 minutes. Stir in boiling water (batter will be thin). Pour into prepared pan.

3. Bake 16 to 18 minutes or until wooden pick inserted in center comes out clean. With knife or metal spatula, loosen cake from edges of pan. Place clean, lint-free dish towel on wire rack; sprinkle lightly with powdered sugar. Invert cake on towel; peel off wax paper. Cool completely.

4. Invert cake, right side up, on cutting board. Cut cake into small rectangles (about 2×1¼ inches). Stir orange peel into whipped topping; spoon dollop on each piece of cake. Garnish as desired. Store ungarnished cake, covered, at room temperature. ■

european mocha fudge cake

1¼ cups (2½ sticks) butter or margarine

¾ cup HERSHEY'S SPECIAL DARK Cocoa

4 eggs

¼ teaspoon salt

1 teaspoon vanilla extract

2 cups sugar

1 cup all-purpose flour

1 cup finely chopped pecans

CREAMY COFFEE FILLING (recipe follows)

Chocolate curls (optional)

1. Heat oven to 350°F. Butter bottom and sides of two 9-inch round baking pans. Line bottoms with wax paper; butter paper.

2. Melt butter in small saucepan; remove from heat. Add cocoa, stirring until blended; cool slightly. Beat eggs in large bowl until foamy; add salt and vanilla. Gradually add sugar, beating well. Add cooled chocolate mixture; blend thoroughly. Fold in flour. Stir in pecans. Pour mixture into prepared pans.

3. Bake 20 to 25 minutes or until wooden pick inserted in centers comes out clean. Do not overbake. Cool 5 minutes; remove from pans to wire racks. Carefully peel off paper. Cool completely. Spread CREAMY COFFEE FILLING between layers, over top and sides of cake. Garnish with chocolate curls, if desired. Refrigerate 1 hour or longer before serving.

CREAMY COFFEE FILLING

1½ cups cold whipping cream

⅓ cup packed light brown sugar

2 teaspoons powdered instant coffee

Combine all ingredients; stir until instant coffee is almost dissolved. Beat until stiff.

MAKES ABOUT 3 CUPS FILLING

MAKE-AHEAD DIRECTIONS

Cooled cake may be wrapped and frozen up to 4 weeks; thaw, wrapped, before filling and frosting. ■

HERSHEY'S lavish chocolate cake

MAKES 12 SERVINGS

1¼ cups all-purpose flour

⅓ cup HERSHEY'S Cocoa

1 teaspoon baking soda

Dash salt

½ cup (1 stick) butter

1 cup sugar

1 cup milk

1 tablespoon white vinegar

½ teaspoon vanilla extract

CHOCOLATE MOUSSE
FILLING (recipe follows)

2 to 4 tablespoons seedless
black raspberry preserves

CHOCOLATE GANACHE
(recipe follows)

Sweetened whipped cream

Fresh raspberries (optional)

Additional HERSHEY'S Cocoa
(optional)

1. Heat oven to 350°F. Line bottom of three 8-inch round baking pans with wax paper. Lightly grease sides of pans. Combine flour, cocoa, baking soda and salt; set aside.

2. Place butter in large microwave-safe bowl. Microwave at MEDIUM (50%) 1 minute or until melted; stir in sugar. Add milk, vinegar and vanilla to butter mixture; stir until blended. Add dry ingredients; whisk until well blended. Pour batter evenly into prepared pans.

3. Bake 15 minutes or until wooden pick inserted in centers comes out clean. Cool 10 minutes. Remove from pans to wire racks; gently peel off wax paper. Cool completely.

4. Prepare CHOCOLATE MOUSSE FILLING. Place one cake layer on serving plate; spread 2 tablespoons preserves over top. Carefully spread half of filling over preserves to within 1 inch of edge. Refrigerate about 10 minutes. Place second layer on top; repeat procedure with remaining preserves and filling. Place remaining layer on top. Refrigerate while preparing CHOCOLATE GANACHE. Spread ganache over top and side of cake.

5. Refrigerate at least 30 minutes. At serving time, garnish with sweetened whipped cream and raspberries; sift cocoa over top. Refrigerate leftover cake.

CHOCOLATE MOUSSE FILLING

1 teaspoon unflavored gelatin

1 tablespoon cold water

2 tablespoons boiling water

½ cup sugar

¼ cup HERSHEY'S Cocoa

1 cup (½ pint) cold whipping cream

1 teaspoon vanilla extract

Sprinkle gelatin over cold water in small bowl; let stand 1 minute to soften. Add boiling water; stir until gelatin is completely dissolved and mixture is clear. Cool slightly. In small mixer bowl, stir together sugar and cocoa; add whipping cream and vanilla. Beat at medium speed of mixer, scraping bottom of bowl occasionally, until stiff; pour in gelatin mixture and beat until well blended. Refrigerate about 20 minutes.

MAKES ABOUT 2 CUPS FILLING

CHOCOLATE GANACHE

Heat 1 cup (½ pint) whipping cream in heavy saucepan over low heat until warm. Add 1½ cups HERSHEY'S SPECIAL DARK Chocolate Chips or HERSHEY'S Semi-Sweet Chocolate Chips; stir constantly just until chips are melted and mixture is smooth. Do not let mixture come to a boil. Transfer mixture to medium bowl; refrigerate until of spreading consistency, about 1½ hours. ■

autumn peanutty carrot cake

MAKES 10 TO 12 SERVINGS

3 eggs

¾ cup vegetable oil

1 teaspoon vanilla extract

1½ cups all-purpose flour

¾ cup granulated sugar

½ cup packed light brown sugar

2 teaspoons ground cinnamon

1¼ teaspoons baking soda

2 cups grated carrots

1⅔ cups (10-ounce package) REESE'S Peanut Butter Chips

½ cup chopped walnuts

CREAM CHEESE FROSTING (recipe follows)

1. Heat oven to 350°F. Grease and flour two 8-inch round baking pans.

2. Beat eggs, oil and vanilla in large bowl. Stir together flour, granulated sugar, brown sugar, cinnamon and baking soda; add to egg mixture and blend well. Stir in carrots, peanut butter chips and walnuts; pour into prepared pans.

3. Bake 30 to 35 minutes or until wooden pick inserted in centers comes out clean. Cool 10 minutes; remove from pans to wire rack. Cool completely. Frost with CREAM CHEESE FROSTING. Cover; refrigerate leftover cake.

CREAM CHEESE FROSTING

Beat 2 packages (3 ounces each) softened cream cheese and ½ cup (1 stick) softened butter until smooth. Gradually add 4 cups powdered sugar and 2 teaspoons vanilla extract, beating until smooth. ■

chocolate syrup swirl cake

MAKES 20 SERVINGS

1 cup (2 sticks) butter or margarine, softened

2 cups sugar

2 teaspoons vanilla extract

3 eggs

2¾ cups all-purpose flour

1¼ teaspoons baking soda, divided

½ teaspoon salt

1 cup buttermilk or sour milk*

1 cup HERSHEY'S Syrup

1 cup MOUNDS Sweetened Coconut Flakes (optional)

*To sour milk: Use 1 tablespoon white vinegar plus milk to equal 1 cup.

1. Heat oven to 350°F. Grease and flour 12-cup fluted tube pan or 10-inch tube pan.

2. Beat butter, sugar and vanilla in large bowl until fluffy. Add eggs; beat well. Stir together flour, 1 teaspoon baking soda and salt; add alternately with buttermilk to butter mixture, beating until well blended.

3. Measure 2 cups batter in small bowl; stir in syrup and remaining ¼ teaspoon baking soda. Add coconut, if desired, to remaining vanilla batter; pour into prepared pan. Pour chocolate batter over vanilla batter in pan; do not mix.

4. Bake 60 to 70 minutes or until wooden pick inserted in center comes out clean. Cool 15 minutes; remove from pan to wire rack. Cool completely; glaze or frost as desired. ■

german black forest cherry torte

⅔ cup unsalted butter

6 eggs

1 cup sugar

1 teaspoon vanilla extract

½ cup all-purpose flour

½ cup HERSHEY'S SPECIAL DARK Cocoa

¼ cup light corn syrup

¼ cup kirsch (cherry brandy)*

2 jars (10 ounces each) maraschino cherries, drained and rinsed

WHIPPED CREAM FILLING AND TOPPING (recipe follows)

*Note: 1 tablespoon almond extract plus 3 tablespoons water can be substituted for kirsch.

1. Heat oven to 350°F. Grease and flour three 8-inch round baking pans.

2. Melt butter over very low heat in small saucepan; remove from heat. Skim off milky solids and discard; reserve remaining butter. Beat eggs, sugar and vanilla on high speed in large bowl until mixture is thick, fluffy and very pale in color (about 10 minutes). Stir together flour and cocoa; sprinkle several tablespoons over top of egg mixture. Gently fold into egg mixture; repeat procedure until all of cocoa mixture is combined with egg mixture. Fold in melted butter, several tablespoons at a time. Divide mixture evenly among prepared pans.

3. Bake 10 to 15 minutes or until wooden pick inserted in centers comes out clean. Cool 5 minutes; with knife, loosen cake from sides of pans. Invert onto wire racks; cool completely.

4. Place cake layers on wax paper; with fork, poke holes about 1-inch apart through all layers. Stir together corn syrup and kirsch; sprinkle evenly over cake layers. Lightly press cherries between layers of paper towels to remove excess moisture. Prepare WHIPPED CREAM FILLING AND TOPPING.

5. To assemble, place one layer on serving plate; spread with ½-inch layer of whipped cream. Place half of drained cherries over top, leaving 1 inch around edge free of cherries; with second layer, repeat procedure. Place third layer on top; frost and garnish top and sides with remaining whipped cream. Cover; refrigerate before serving. Garnish as desired.

WHIPPED CREAM FILLING AND TOPPING

In large mixer bowl, beat 3 cups (1½ pints) cold whipping cream, ½ cup powdered sugar and 1 teaspoon almond extract until stiff. Cover; refrigerate until ready to use. ■

chocolate lemon marble cake

MAKES 16 TO 18 SERVINGS

2½ cups all-purpose flour

1¾ cups plus ⅓ cup sugar, divided

2 teaspoons baking powder

1¼ teaspoons baking soda, divided

½ teaspoon salt

⅓ cup butter or margarine, softened

⅓ cup shortening

3 eggs

1⅔ cups buttermilk or sour milk*

2 teaspoons vanilla extract

⅓ cup HERSHEY'S Cocoa

¼ cup water

2 teaspoons freshly grated lemon peel

¼ teaspoon lemon juice

COCOA GLAZE (recipe follows)

*To sour milk: Use 1 tablespoon plus 2 teaspoons white vinegar plus milk to equal 1⅔ cups.

1. Heat oven to 375°F. Grease and flour 12-cup fluted tube pan.**

2. Stir together flour, 1¾ cups sugar, baking powder, 1 teaspoon baking soda and salt in large bowl. Add butter, shortening, eggs, buttermilk and vanilla; beat on medium speed of electric mixer 3 minutes.

3. Stir together cocoa, remaining ⅓ cup sugar, remaining ¼ teaspoon baking soda and water; blend into ⅔ cup vanilla batter. Blend lemon peel and lemon juice into remaining vanilla batter; drop spoonfuls of lemon batter into prepared pan. Drop spoonfuls of chocolate batter on top of lemon batter; swirl with knife or metal spatula for marbled effect.

4. Bake 35 to 40 minutes or until wooden pick inserted in center comes out clean. Cool 15 minutes; remove from pan to wire rack. Cool completely. Glaze with COCOA GLAZE.

Cake may also be baked in two 9×5× 3-inch loaf pans. Bake 40 to 45 minutes or until wooden pick inserted in centers comes out clean.

COCOA GLAZE

¼ cup HERSHEY'S Cocoa

3 tablespoons light corn syrup

4 teaspoons water

½ teaspoon vanilla extract

1 cup powdered sugar

Combine cocoa, corn syrup and water in small saucepan; cook over medium heat, stirring constantly, until mixture thickens. Remove from heat; blend in vanilla and powdered sugar. Beat until smooth. ■

chocolate almond torte

4 eggs, separated

¾ cup sugar, divided

¾ cup ground blanched almonds

⅓ cup all-purpose flour

⅓ cup HERSHEY'S Cocoa

½ teaspoon baking soda

¼ teaspoon salt

¼ cup water

1 teaspoon vanilla extract

¼ teaspoon almond extract

CHERRY FILLING
(recipe follows)

CHOCOLATE GLAZE
(recipe follows)

Sliced almonds, maraschino cherries or candied cherries, halved

1. Heat oven to 375°F. Grease bottoms of three 8-inch round baking pans. Line bottoms with wax paper; grease paper.

2. Beat egg yolks on medium speed of mixer 3 minutes in medium bowl. Gradually add ½ cup sugar; continue beating 2 minutes. Stir together almonds, flour, cocoa, baking soda and salt; add alternately with water to egg yolk mixture, beating on low speed just until blended. Stir in vanilla and almond extract.

3. Beat egg whites in large bowl until foamy; gradually add remaining ¼ cup sugar, beating until stiff peaks form. Fold small amount beaten egg whites into chocolate mixture; gently fold chocolate mixture into remaining whites just until blended. Spread batter evenly in prepared pans.

4. Bake 16 to 18 minutes or until top springs back when touched lightly in center. Cool 10 minutes; remove from pans to wire racks. Cool completely.

5. Prepare CHERRY FILLING. Place one cake layer on serving plate; spread half of filling over top. Repeat, ending with plain layer on top. Prepare CHOCOLATE GLAZE; spread on top of cake, allowing glaze to run down sides. Garnish with almonds and cherry halves. Refrigerate until glaze is set. Cover; refrigerate leftover torte.

CHERRY FILLING

1 cup (½ pint) cold whipping cream

¼ cup powdered sugar

1½ teaspoons kirsch (cherry brandy) or ¼ teaspoon almond extract

⅓ cup chopped red candied cherries

Beat whipping cream, powdered sugar and brandy until stiff; fold in cherries.

MAKES ABOUT 2 CUPS FILLING

CHOCOLATE GLAZE

1 tablespoon butter or margarine

2 tablespoons HERSHEY'S Cocoa

2 tablespoons water

1 cup powdered sugar

¼ teaspoon vanilla extract

Melt butter in small saucepan over low heat; add cocoa and water, stirring constantly until slightly thickened. Remove from heat; gradually add powdered sugar and vanilla, beating with whisk until smooth and of spreading consistency. Add additional water, ½ teaspoon at a time, if needed.

MAKES ABOUT ¾ CUP GLAZE ■

strawberry chocolate chip shortcake

MAKES 12 SERVINGS

1 cup sugar, divided

½ cup (1 stick) butter or margarine, softened

1 egg

2 teaspoons vanilla extract, divided

1½ cups all-purpose flour

½ teaspoon baking powder

1 cup HERSHEY'S Mini Chips Semi-Sweet Chocolate, HERSHEY'S SPECIAL DARK Chocolate Chips or HERSHEY'S Semi-Sweet Chocolate Chips, divided

1 container (16 ounces) dairy sour cream

2 eggs

2 cups frozen non-dairy whipped topping, thawed

Fresh strawberries, rinsed and halved

1. Heat oven to 350°F. Grease 9-inch springform pan.

2. Beat ½ cup sugar and butter in large bowl. Add 1 egg and 1 teaspoon vanilla; beat until creamy. Gradually add flour and baking powder, beating until smooth; stir in ½ cup small chocolate chips. Press mixture onto bottom of prepared pan.

3. Stir together sour cream, remaining ½ cup sugar, 2 eggs and remaining 1 teaspoon vanilla in medium bowl; stir in remaining ½ cup small chocolate chips. Pour over mixture in pan.

4. Bake 50 to 55 minutes until almost set in center and edges are lightly browned. Cool completely on wire rack; remove side of pan. Spread whipped topping over top. Cover; refrigerate. Just before serving, arrange strawberry halves on top of cake; garnish as desired. Refrigerate leftover dessert. ■

HERSHEY'S SPECIAL DARK
snack cake medley

MAKES 12 TO 16 SERVINGS

CREAM CHEESE FILLING
(recipe follows)

3 cups all-purpose flour

2 cups sugar

⅔ cup HERSHEY'S Cocoa

2 teaspoons baking soda

1 teaspoon salt

2 cups water

⅔ cup vegetable oil

2 eggs

2 tablespoons white vinegar

2 teaspoons vanilla extract

½ cup HERSHEY'S SPECIAL DARK
Chocolate Chips

½ cup MOUNDS Sweetened
Coconut Flakes

½ cup chopped nuts

1. Heat oven to 350°F. Grease and flour 13×9×2-inch baking pan. Prepare CREAM CHEESE FILLING; set aside.

2. Stir together flour, sugar, cocoa, baking soda and salt in large bowl. Add water, oil, eggs, vinegar and vanilla; beat on medium speed of mixer 2 minutes or until well blended. Pour 3 cups batter into prepared pan. Gently drop cream cheese filling onto batter by heaping teaspoonfuls. Carefully spoon remaining batter over filling. Combine chocolate chips, coconut and nuts; sprinkle over top of batter.

3. Bake 50 to 55 minutes or until wooden pick inserted into cake center comes out almost clean and cake starts to crack slightly. Cool completely in pan on wire rack. Cover and store leftover cake in refrigerator.

CREAM CHEESE FILLING

½ cup HERSHEY'S SPECIAL DARK Chocolate Chips

1 package (8 ounces) cream cheese, softened

⅓ cup sugar

1 egg

½ teaspoon vanilla extract

1. Place chocolate chips in small microwave-safe bowl. Microwave at MEDIUM (50%) 30 seconds; stir. If necessary, microwave an additional 10 seconds at a time, stirring after each heating, until chips are melted and smooth when stirred.

2. Beat cream cheese and sugar in medium bowl until well blended. Beat in egg and vanilla. Add melted chocolate, beating until well blended. ■

HERSHEY'S "PERFECTLY CHOCOLATE" Chocolate Cake

MAKES 10 TO 12 SERVINGS

2 cups sugar

1¾ cups all-purpose flour

¾ cup HERSHEY'S Cocoa

1½ teaspoons baking powder

1½ teaspoons baking soda

1 teaspoon salt

2 eggs

1 cup milk

½ cup vegetable oil

2 teaspoons vanilla extract

1 cup boiling water

"PERFECTLY CHOCOLATE" CHOCOLATE FROSTING (recipe follows)

1. Heat oven to 350°F. Grease and flour two 9-inch round baking pans.

2. Stir together sugar, flour, cocoa, baking powder, baking soda and salt in large bowl. Add eggs, milk, oil and vanilla; beat on medium speed of mixer 2 minutes. Stir in boiling water (batter will be thin). Pour batter evenly into prepared pans.

3. Bake 30 to 35 minutes or until wooden pick inserted into centers comes out clean. Cool 10 minutes; remove from pans to wire racks. Cool completely. Frost with "PERFECTLY CHOCOLATE" Chocolate Frosting.

One-Pan Cake: Grease and flour 13×9×2-inch baking pan. Heat oven to 350°F. Pour batter into prepared pan. Bake 35 to 40 minutes. Cool completely. Frost.

Three Layer Cake: Grease and flour three 8-inch round baking pans. Heat oven to 350°F. Pour batter into prepared pans. Bake 30 to 35 minutes. Cool 10 minutes; remove from pans to wire racks. Cool completely. Frost.

Bundt Cake: Grease and flour 12-cup fluted tube pan. Heat oven to 350°F. Pour batter into prepared pan. Bake 50 to 55 minutes. Cool 15 minutes; remove from pan to wire rack. Cool completely. Frost.

Cupcakes: Line muffin cups (2½ inches in diameter) with paper bake cups. Heat oven to 350°F. Fill cups ⅔ full with batter. Bake 22 to 25 minutes. Cool completely. Frost. About 30 cupcakes.

Dip knife or spatula in ice water before frosting cake—it will frost easier and keep the cake from breaking up.

"PERFECTLY CHOCOLATE" CHOCOLATE FROSTING

½ cup (1 stick) butter or margarine

⅔ cup HERSHEY'S Cocoa

3 cups powdered sugar

⅓ cup milk

1 teaspoon vanilla extract

Melt butter. Stir in cocoa. Alternately add powdered sugar and milk, beating to spreading consistency. Add small amount additional milk, if needed. Stir in vanilla.

MAKES ABOUT 2 CUPS FROSTING ■

T A S T Y

CHEESECAKES

IMMERSE YOURSELF

chilled raspberry cheesecake

MAKES 10 TO 12 SERVINGS

1½ cups vanilla wafer crumbs (about 45 wafers, crushed)

⅓ cup HERSHEY'S Cocoa

⅓ cup powdered sugar

⅓ cup butter or margarine, melted

1 package (10 ounces) frozen raspberries, thawed

1 envelope unflavored gelatin

½ cup cold water

½ cup boiling water

2 packages (8 ounces each) cream cheese, softened

½ cup granulated sugar

1 teaspoon vanilla extract

3 tablespoons seedless red raspberry preserves

CHOCOLATE WHIPPED CREAM (recipe follows)

1. Heat oven to 350°F.

2. Stir together crumbs, ⅓ cup cocoa and ⅓ cup powdered sugar in medium bowl; stir in melted butter. Press mixture onto bottom and 1½ inches up side of 9-inch springform pan. Bake 10 minutes; cool completely.

3. Purée and strain raspberries; set aside. Sprinkle gelatin over cold water in small bowl; let stand several minutes to soften. Add boiling water; stir until gelatin dissolves completely and mixture is clear. Beat cream cheese, granulated sugar and 1 teaspoon vanilla in large bowl until smooth. Gradually add raspberry purée and gelatin, mixing thoroughly; pour into prepared crust.

4. Refrigerate several hours or overnight. Loosen cake from side of pan with knife; remove side of pan. Spread raspberry preserves over top. Garnish with CHOCOLATE WHIPPED CREAM. Cover; refrigerate leftovers.

CHOCOLATE WHIPPED CREAM

Stir together ½ cup powdered sugar and ¼ cup HERSHEY'S Cocoa in medium bowl. Add 1 cup cold whipping cream and 1 teaspoon vanilla extract; beat until stiff. ■

cappuccino-KISSed cheesecake

MAKES 16 SERVINGS

1½ cups chocolate cookie crumbs

6 tablespoons butter or margarine, melted

1¼ cups HERSHEY'S MINI KISSES BRAND Milk Chocolates, divided

4 packages (8 ounces each) cream cheese, softened

⅔ cup sugar

3 eggs

⅓ cup milk

1 tablespoon instant espresso powder

¼ teaspoon ground cinnamon

ESPRESSO CREAM (recipe follows)

1. Heat oven to 350°F. Combine cookie crumbs and butter; press onto bottom and 1 inch up side of 9-inch springform pan.

2. Melt 1 cup chocolate pieces in small saucepan over low heat, stirring constantly. Combine cream cheese and sugar in large bowl, beating on medium speed of mixer until well blended. Add eggs, milk, espresso powder and cinnamon; beat on low speed until well blended. Add melted chocolate pieces; beat on medium 2 minutes. Spoon mixture into crust.

3. Bake 55 minutes. Remove from oven to wire rack. Cool 15 minutes; with knife, loosen cake from side of pan. Cool completely; remove side of pan. Cover; refrigerate at least 4 hours before serving.

4. To serve, garnish with ESPRESSO CREAM and remaining ¼ cup chocolates. Cover; refrigerate leftover cheesecake.

ESPRESSO CREAM

Beat ½ cup cold whipping cream, 2 tablespoons powdered sugar and 1 teaspoon instant espresso powder until stiff. ■

peanut butter holiday cheesecake

MAKES 12 TO 14 SERVINGS

6 tablespoons butter or margarine, melted

6 tablespoons HERSHEY'S Cocoa

⅓ cup powdered sugar

1½ cups (about 45 cookies) vanilla wafer cookie crumbs

1 package (8 ounces) cream cheese, softened

2 tablespoons lemon juice

1½ cups REESE'S Peanut Butter Chips

1 can (14 ounces) sweetened condensed milk (not evaporated milk)

1 cup (½ pint) whipping cream, whipped

CRANBERRY TOPPING (recipe follows)

1. Stir together butter, cocoa, powdered sugar and vanilla wafer crumbs in bowl. Press firmly onto bottom of 9-inch springform pan; refrigerate while preparing filling.

2. Beat cream cheese and lemon juice in large bowl until fluffy; set aside. Combine peanut butter chips and sweetened condensed milk in medium saucepan over low heat; stir constantly until chips are melted and mixture is smooth. Add to cream cheese mixture; blend well. Fold in whipped cream. Pour evenly over crumb crust.

3. Cover; refrigerate while preparing CRANBERRY TOPPING. Spread topping evenly over cheesecake. Cover; refrigerate several hours or overnight. Remove side of springform pan to serve. Cover; refrigerate leftover cheesecake.

CRANBERRY TOPPING

2 cups fresh or frozen cranberries

1 cup sugar

¾ cup water, divided

2 tablespoons cornstarch

1 teaspoon vanilla extract

1. Stir together cranberries, sugar and ½ cup water in medium saucepan. Cook over medium heat, stirring occasionally, until mixture comes to a boil. Reduce heat; simmer 3 minutes. Remove from heat.

2. Stir together cornstarch and remaining ¼ cup water; gradually add to cranberry mixture. Return to heat; stir constantly until mixture thickens and resembles fruit preserves (about 4 minutes). Cool to room temperature; stir in vanilla.

MAKES ABOUT 3½ CUPS TOPPING ■

HERSHEY'S SPECIAL DARK
chocolate layered cheesecake

MAKES 10 TO 12 SERVINGS

CHOCOLATE CRUMB CRUST
(recipe follows)

3 packages (8 ounces each) cream cheese, softened

¾ cup sugar

4 eggs

¼ cup heavy cream

2 teaspoons vanilla extract

¼ teaspoon salt

2 cups (12-ounce package) HERSHEY'S SPECIAL DARK Chocolate Chips, divided

½ teaspoon shortening (do not use butter, margarine, spread or oil)

1. Prepare CHOCOLATE CRUMB CRUST. Heat oven to 350°F.

2. Beat cream cheese and sugar in large bowl until smooth. Gradually beat in eggs, heavy cream, vanilla and salt, beating until well blended; set aside.

3. Set aside 2 tablespoons chocolate chips. Place remaining chips in large microwave-safe bowl. Microwave at MEDIUM (50%) 1½ minutes; stir. If necessary, microwave at MEDIUM an additional 15 seconds at a time, stirring after each heating, until chocolate is melted when stirred.

4. Gradually blend 1½ cups cheesecake batter into melted chocolate. Spread 2 cups chocolate mixture in prepared crust.

5. Blend another 2 cups plain cheesecake batter into remaining chocolate mixture; spread 2 cups of this mixture over first layer. Stir remaining cheesecake batter into remaining chocolate mixture; spread over second layer.

6. Bake 50 to 55 minutes or until center is almost set. Remove from oven to wire rack. With knife, immediately loosen cake from side of pan. Cool to room temperature.

7. Place reserved chocolate chips and shortening in small microwave-safe bowl. Microwave at MEDIUM 30 seconds; stir. If necessary, microwave at MEDIUM an additional 10 seconds at a time, stirring after each heating, until chocolate is melted and smooth when stirred. Drizzle over top of cheesecake. Cover; refrigerate several hours until cold. Cover and refrigerate leftover cheesecake.

CHOCOLATE CRUMB CRUST

Stir together 1½ cups vanilla wafer crumbs (about 45 wafers), ½ cup powdered sugar and ¼ cup HERSHEY'S Cocoa; stir in ¼ cup (½ stick) melted butter or margarine. Press mixture onto bottom and 1½ inches up sides of 9-inch springform pan. ■

triple layer cheesecake

MAKES 12 TO 14 SERVINGS

CHOCOLATE CRUMB CRUST
(recipe follows)

3 packages (8 ounces each)
cream cheese, softened

¾ cup sugar

3 eggs

⅓ cup dairy sour cream

3 tablespoons all-purpose flour

1 teaspoon vanilla extract

¼ teaspoon salt

1 cup HERSHEY'S Butterscotch
Chips, melted*

1 cup HERSHEY'S Premier White
Chips, melted*

1 cup HERSHEY'S SPECIAL DARK
Chocolate Chips or HERSHEY'S
Semi-Sweet Chocolate Chips,
melted*

TRIPLE DRIZZLE
(recipe follows, optional)

***To melt chips: Place chips in
separate medium microwave-
safe bowls. Microwave at MEDIUM
(50%) 1 minute; stir. If necessary,
microwave at MEDIUM an additional
15 seconds at a time, stirring after
each heating, just until chips are
melted when stirred.**

1. Heat oven to 350°F. Prepare CHOCOLATE CRUMB CRUST.

2. Beat cream cheese and sugar in large bowl on medium speed of mixer until smooth. Add eggs, sour cream, flour, vanilla and salt; beat until blended. Stir 1⅓ cups batter into melted butterscotch chips until smooth; pour into prepared crust. Stir 1⅓ cups batter into melted white chips until smooth; pour over butterscotch layer. Stir remaining batter into melted chocolate chips until smooth; pour over white layer.

3. Bake 55 to 60 minutes or until almost set in center. Remove from oven to wire rack. With knife, immediately loosen cake from side of pan. Cool completely; remove side of pan. Prepare TRIPLE DRIZZLE, if desired; drizzle, one flavor at a time, over top of cheesecake. Refrigerate about 3 hours. Cover; refrigerate leftover cheesecake.

CHOCOLATE CRUMB CRUST

Heat oven to 350°F. Stir together 1½ cups vanilla wafer crumbs (about 45 wafers), ½ cup powdered sugar and ¼ cup HERSHEY'S Cocoa; stir in ⅓ cup melted butter or margarine. Press mixture onto bottom and 1½ inches up side of 9-inch springform pan. Bake 8 minutes. Cool.

Use cocoa for delicious chocolate cakes, frosting, brownies and hot cocoa—also a perfect garnish for baked desserts.

TRIPLE DRIZZLE

1 tablespoon each HERSHEY'S Butterscotch Chips, HERSHEY'S Semi-Sweet Chocolate Chips* and HERSHEY'S Premier White Chips

1½ teaspoons shortening (do not use butter, margarine, spread or oil), divided

*Substitute 1 tablespoon HERSHEY'S SPECIAL DARK Chocolate Chips for HERSHEY'S Semi-Sweet Chocolate Chips, if desired

Place 1 tablespoon HERSHEY'S Butterscotch Chips and ½ teaspoon shortening (do not use butter, margarine, spread or oil) in small microwave-safe bowl. Microwave at MEDIUM (50%) 30 to 45 seconds; stir. If necessary, microwave an additional 15 seconds at a time, stirring after each heating, just until chips are melted when stirred. Repeat procedure with 1 tablespoon HERSHEY'S Semi-Sweet Chocolate Chips and 1 tablespoon HERSHEY'S Premier White Chips. ■

HERSHEY'S SPECIAL DARK
truffle brownie cheesecake

MAKES 10 TO 12 SERVINGS

BROWNIE LAYER

6 tablespoons melted butter or margarine

1¼ cups sugar

1 teaspoon vanilla extract

2 eggs

1 cup plus 2 tablespoons all-purpose flour

⅓ cup HERSHEY'S Cocoa

½ teaspoon baking powder

½ teaspoon salt

TRUFFLE CHEESECAKE LAYER

3 packages (8 ounces each) cream cheese, softened

¾ cup sugar

4 eggs

¼ cup heavy cream

2 teaspoons vanilla extract

¼ teaspoon salt

2 cups (12-ounce package) HERSHEY'S SPECIAL DARK Chocolate Chips, divided

½ teaspoon shortening (do not use butter, margarine, spread or oil)

1. Heat oven to 350°F. Grease 9-inch springform pan.

2. For BROWNIE LAYER, stir together melted butter, 1¼ cups sugar and 1 teaspoon vanilla. Add 2 eggs; stir until blended. Stir in flour, cocoa, baking powder and ½ teaspoon salt; blend well. Spread in prepared pan. Bake 25 to 30 minutes or until brownie layer pulls away from sides of pan.

3. Meanwhile for TRUFFLE CHEESECAKE LAYER, beat cream cheese and ¾ cup sugar with electric mixer on medium speed in large bowl until smooth. Gradually beat in 4 eggs, heavy cream, 2 teaspoons vanilla and ¼ teaspoon salt until well blended.

4. Set aside 2 tablespoons chocolate chips. Place remaining chips in large microwave-safe bowl. Microwave at MEDIUM (50%) 1½ minutes or until chips are melted and smooth when stirred. Gradually blend melted chocolate into cheesecake batter.

5. Remove BROWNIE LAYER from oven and immediately spoon cheesecake mixture over brownie. Return to oven; continue baking 45 to 50 minutes or until center is almost set. Remove from oven to wire rack. With knife, loosen cake from side of pan. Cool to room temperature. Remove side of pan.

6. Place remaining 2 tablespoons chocolate chips and shortening in small microwave-safe bowl. Microwave at MEDIUM (50%) 30 seconds or until chips are melted and mixture is smooth when stirred. Drizzle over top of cheesecake. Cover; refrigerate several hours until cold. Garnish as desired. Cover and refrigerate leftover cheesecake. ■

creamy ambrosia cheesecake

MAKES 10 TO 12 SERVINGS

1⅓ cups graham cracker crumbs

½ cup MOUNDS Sweetened Coconut Flakes

¼ cup (½ stick) melted butter or margarine

1¼ cups plus 2 tablespoons sugar, divided

1 can (11 ounces) mandarin orange segments

1 can (8 ounces) crushed pineapple in juice

3 packages (8 ounces each) cream cheese, softened

3 eggs

2 cups (12-ounce package) HERSHEY'S Premier White Chips

TROPICAL FRUIT SAUCE (recipe follows)

Additional MOUNDS Sweetened Coconut Flakes, optional

1. Heat oven to 350°F. Stir graham cracker crumbs, coconut, melted butter and 2 tablespoons sugar in medium bowl. Press mixture firmly onto bottom of 9-inch springform pan. Bake 8 minutes; cool slightly. Drain oranges and pineapple, reserving juices. Chop oranges into small pieces.

2. Beat cream cheese in large bowl until fluffy. Add remaining 1¼ cups sugar; beat well. Add eggs; beat well. Stir in white chips, oranges and pineapple. Pour mixture over crust.

3. Bake 60 to 65 minutes or until center is almost set. Remove from oven to wire rack. With knife, loosen cake from side of pan. Cool completely; remove side of pan. Cover; refrigerate until cold. Serve with TROPICAL FRUIT SAUCE. Garnish with additional coconut, if desired. Cover and refrigerate leftovers.

TROPICAL FRUIT SAUCE

Juice drained from canned mandarin oranges

Juice drained from canned crushed pineapple

¼ cup sugar

1 tablespoon cornstarch

¼ teaspoon orange extract or pineapple extract

Combine fruit juices; pour 1 cup combined juice into medium saucepan and discard any remaining juices. Stir in sugar and cornstarch. Cook over medium heat, stirring constantly, until thickened. Remove from heat. Stir in orange extract or pineapple extract. Cool to room temperature before serving. Cover and refrigerate leftover sauce.

MAKES ABOUT ¾ CUP SAUCE ■

ultra
chocolate cheesecake

MAKES 12 SERVINGS

MOCHA CRUMB CRUST
(recipe follows)

3 packages (8 ounces each)
cream cheese, softened

1¼ cups sugar

1 container (8 ounces) dairy
sour cream

2 teaspoons vanilla extract

½ cup HERSHEY'S Cocoa

2 tablespoons all-purpose flour

3 eggs

CHOCOLATE DRIZZLE
(recipe follows)

1. Prepare MOCHA CRUMB CRUST. Heat oven to 350°F.

2. Beat cream cheese and sugar in large bowl until fluffy. Add sour cream and vanilla; beat until blended. Add cocoa and flour; beat until blended. Add eggs; beat well. Pour into crust.

3. Bake 50 to 55 minutes or until set. Remove from oven to wire rack. With knife, loosen cake from side of pan. Cool completely; remove side of pan. Prepare CHOCOLATE DRIZZLE; drizzle over top. Refrigerate 4 to 6 hours. Cover; refrigerate leftover cheesecake.

MOCHA CRUMB CRUST

1¼ cups vanilla wafer crumbs

¼ cup sugar

¼ cup HERSHEY'S Cocoa

1 teaspoon powdered instant espresso or coffee

⅓ cup butter, melted

Heat oven to 350°F. Stir together crumbs, sugar, cocoa and instant espresso in medium bowl. Add butter; stir until well blended. Press mixture firmly onto bottom and 1-inch up side of 9-inch springform pan. Bake 8 minutes; cool slightly.

CHOCOLATE DRIZZLE

Place ½ cup HERSHEY'S SPECIAL DARK Chocolate Chips or HERSHEY'S Semi-Sweet Chocolate Chips and 2 teaspoons shortening (do not use butter, margarine, spread or oil) in small microwave-safe bowl. Microwave at MEDIUM (50%) 30 seconds; stir. If necessary, microwave at MEDIUM an additional 10 seconds at a time, stirring after each heating, just until chips are melted and mixture is smooth. ■

ENTICING
PIES & TARTS

Savor the Flavor

fudge-bottomed chocolate layer pie

MAKES 6 TO 8 SERVINGS

1 cup HERSHEY'S SPECIAL DARK Chocolate Chips, divided

2 tablespoons plus ¼ cup milk, divided

1 packaged chocolate crumb crust (6 ounces)

1½ cups miniature marshmallows

1 tub (8 ounces) frozen nondairy whipped topping, thawed and divided

Additional sweetened whipped cream or whipped topping (optional)

1. Place ⅓ cup chocolate chips and 2 tablespoons milk in microwave-safe bowl. Microwave 30 seconds at MEDIUM (50%); stir. If necessary, microwave an additional 15 seconds at a time, stirring after each heating, until chips are melted and mixture is smooth when stirred. Spread on bottom of crust. Refrigerate while preparing next step.

2. Place marshmallows, remaining ⅔ cup chocolate chips and remaining ¼ cup milk in small saucepan. Cook over medium heat, stirring constantly, until marshmallows are melted and mixture is well blended. Transfer to separate large bowl; cool completely.

3. Stir 2 cups whipped topping into cooled chocolate mixture; spread 2 cups mixture over chocolate in crust. Blend remaining whipped topping and remaining chocolate mixture; spread over surface of pie.

4. Cover; freeze several hours or until firm. Garnish as desired. Cover and freeze leftover pie. ■

all-chocolate boston cream pie

MAKES 8 SERVINGS

1 cup all-purpose flour

1 cup sugar

⅓ cup HERSHEY'S Cocoa

½ teaspoon baking soda

6 tablespoons butter or margarine, softened

1 cup milk

1 egg

1 teaspoon vanilla extract

CHOCOLATE FILLING (recipe follows)

SATINY CHOCOLATE GLAZE (recipe follows)

1. Heat oven to 350°F. Grease and flour one 9-inch round baking pan.

2. Stir together flour, sugar, cocoa and baking soda in large bowl. Add butter, milk, egg and vanilla. Beat on low speed of mixer until all ingredients are moistened. Beat on medium speed 2 minutes. Pour batter into prepared pan.

3. Bake 30 to 35 minutes or until wooden pick inserted in center comes out clean. Cool 10 minutes; remove from pan to wire rack. Cool completely. Prepare CHOCOLATE FILLING. Cut cake into two thin layers. Place one layer on serving plate; spread filling over layer. Top with remaining layer.

4. Prepare SATINY CHOCOLATE GLAZE. Pour onto top of cake, allowing some to drizzle down sides. Refrigerate until serving time. Cover; refrigerate leftover cake.

CHOCOLATE FILLING

½ cup sugar

¼ cup HERSHEY'S Cocoa

2 tablespoons cornstarch

1½ cups light cream

1 tablespoon butter or margarine

1 teaspoon vanilla extract

Stir together sugar, cocoa and cornstarch in medium saucepan; gradually stir in light cream. Cook over medium heat, stirring constantly, until mixture thickens and begins to boil. Boil 1 minute, stirring constantly; remove from heat. Stir in butter and vanilla. Press plastic wrap directly onto surface. Cool completely.

SATINY CHOCOLATE GLAZE

2 tablespoons water

1 tablespoon butter or margarine

1 tablespoon corn syrup

2 tablespoons HERSHEY'S Cocoa

¾ cup powdered sugar

½ teaspoon vanilla extract

Heat water, butter and corn syrup in small saucepan to boiling. Remove from heat; immediately stir in cocoa. With whisk, gradually beat in powdered sugar and vanilla until smooth; cool slightly. ■

peanut butter and milk chocolate chip cookie pie

MAKES 8 TO 10 SERVINGS

½ cup (1 stick) butter or margarine, softened

2 eggs, beaten

2 teaspoons vanilla extract

1 cup sugar

½ cup all-purpose flour

1 cup HERSHEY'S Milk Chocolate Chips

1 cup REESE'S Peanut Butter Chips

1 cup chopped pecans or walnuts

1 unbaked (9-inch) pie crust

Sweetened whipped cream or ice cream (optional)

1. Heat oven to 350°F.

2. Beat butter in medium bowl; add eggs and vanilla. Stir together sugar and flour; add to butter mixture. Stir in milk chocolate chips, peanut butter chips and nuts; pour into unbaked pie crust.

3. Bake 50 to 55 minutes or until golden brown. Cool about 1 hour on wire rack; serve warm with sweetened whipped cream or ice cream, if desired.

TO REHEAT

One slice at time, microwave at HIGH (100%) 10 to 15 seconds. ■

chocolate and vanilla-swirled cheese pie

MAKES 8 SERVINGS

2 packages (8 ounces each) cream cheese, softened

½ cup sugar

1 teaspoon vanilla extract

2 eggs

1 prepared deep-dish crumb crust (9 ounces)

1 cup HERSHEY'S SPECIAL DARK Chocolate Chips

¼ cup milk

Red raspberry jam (optional)

1. Heat oven to 350°F.

2. Beat cream cheese, sugar and vanilla in mixer bowl until well blended. Add eggs; mix thoroughly. Spread 2 cups batter in crumb crust.

3. Place chocolate chips in medium microwave-safe bowl. Microwave at MEDIUM (50%) 1 minute; stir. If necessary, microwave an additional 15 seconds at a time, stirring after each heating, until chocolate is melted and smooth when stirred. Cool slightly. Add melted chocolate and milk to remaining batter; blend thoroughly. Drop chocolate batter by tablespoonfuls onto vanilla batter. Gently swirl with knife for marbled effect.

4. Bake 30 to 35 minutes or until center is almost set. Cool; refrigerate several hours or overnight. Drizzle with warmed red raspberry jam, if desired. Cover and refrigerate leftover pie. ■

classic chocolate cream pie

MAKES 8 TO 10 SERVINGS

5 sections (½ ounce each)
HERSHEY'S Unsweetened
Chocolate Premium Baking Bar,
broken into pieces

3 cups milk, divided

1⅓ cups sugar

3 tablespoons all-purpose flour

3 tablespoons cornstarch

½ teaspoon salt

3 egg yolks

2 tablespoons butter or margarine

1½ teaspoons vanilla extract

1 baked (9-inch) pie crust,
cooled, or 1 prepared (9-inch)
crumb crust

Sweetened whipped
cream (optional)

When whipping cream, keep cream, bowl and utensils as cold as possible— the cream will whip more easily and create a larger volume.

1. Combine chocolate and 2 cups milk in medium saucepan; cook over medium heat, stirring constantly, just until mixture boils. Remove from heat and set aside.

2. Stir together sugar, flour, cornstarch and salt in medium bowl. Whisk remaining 1 cup milk into egg yolks in separate bowl; stir into sugar mixture. Gradually add to chocolate mixture. Cook over medium heat, whisking constantly, until mixture boils; boil and stir 1 minute. Remove from heat; stir in butter and vanilla.

3. Pour into prepared crust; press plastic wrap directly onto surface. Cool; refrigerate until well chilled. Top with whipped cream, if desired. ∎

white chip fruit tart

MAKES 10 TO 12 SERVINGS

¾ cup (1½ sticks) butter or margarine, softened

½ cup powdered sugar

1½ cups all-purpose flour

2 cups (12-ounce package) HERSHEY'S Premier White Chips

¼ cup whipping cream

1 package (8 ounces) cream cheese, softened

FRUIT TOPPING (recipe follows)

Assorted fresh fruit, sliced

1. Heat oven to 300°F.

2. Beat butter and powdered sugar in small bowl until smooth; blend in flour. Press mixture onto bottom and up side of 12-inch round pizza pan. Flute edge, if desired.

3. Bake 20 to 25 minutes or until lightly browned; cool completely.

4. Place white chips and whipping cream in medium microwave-safe bowl. Microwave at MEDIUM (50%) 1 to 1½ minutes or until chips are melted and mixture is smooth when stirred. Beat in cream cheese. Spread on cooled crust. Prepare FRUIT TOPPING. Arrange fruit over chip mixture; carefully pour or brush topping over fruit. Cover; refrigerate assembled tart until just before serving.

FRUIT TOPPING

¼ cup sugar

1 tablespoon cornstarch

½ cup pineapple juice

½ teaspoon lemon juice

Stir together sugar and cornstarch in small saucepan; stir in juices. Cook over medium heat, stirring constantly, until thickened; cool. ■

chocolate chip cookie dough cheesepie

MAKES 8 SERVINGS

COOKIE DOUGH
(recipe follows)

2 packages (3 ounces each)
cream cheese, softened

⅓ cup sugar

⅓ cup dairy sour cream

1 egg

½ teaspoon vanilla extract

1 packaged chocolate crumb crust
(6 ounces)

1. Prepare COOKIE DOUGH.

2. Heat oven to 350°F.

3. Beat cream cheese and sugar in small bowl on medium speed of mixer until smooth; blend in sour cream, egg and vanilla. Pour into crust. Drop COOKIE DOUGH by teaspoons evenly onto cream cheese mixture.

4. Bake 35 to 40 minutes or just until almost set in center. Cool completely on wire rack. Cover; refrigerate leftover pie.

COOKIE DOUGH

2 tablespoons butter or margarine, softened

¼ cup packed light brown sugar

¼ cup all-purpose flour

1 tablespoon water

¼ teaspoon vanilla extract

1 cup HERSHEY'S SPECIAL DARK Chocolate Chips or HERSHEY'S Semi-Sweet Chocolate Chips

Beat butter and brown sugar in small bowl until fluffy. Add flour, water and vanilla; beat until blended. Stir in chocolate chips. ■

crispy chocolate ice cream mud pie

MAKES 8 SERVINGS

½ cup HERSHEY'S Syrup or HERSHEY'S WHOPPERS Chocolate Malt Syrup, divided

⅓ cup HERSHEY'S SPECIAL DARK Chocolate Chips or HERSHEY'S Semi-Sweet Chocolate Chips

2 cups crisp rice cereal

4 cups (1 quart) vanilla ice cream, divided

4 cups (1 quart) chocolate ice cream, divided

Additional HERSHEY'S Syrup or HERSHEY'S WHOPPERS Chocolate Syrup

1. Butter 9-inch pie plate.

2. Place ½ cup chocolate syrup and chocolate chips in medium microwave-safe bowl. Microwave at MEDIUM (50%) 45 seconds or until hot; stir until smooth. Reserve ¼ cup chocolate syrup mixture; set aside. Add cereal to remaining chocolate mixture, stirring until well coated; cool slightly.

3. Press cereal mixture, using back of spoon, evenly on bottom and up sides of prepared pie plate to form crust. Place in freezer 15 to 20 minutes or until crust is firm. Spread half of vanilla ice cream into crust; spoon reserved ¼ cup chocolate syrup mixture over layer. Spread half of chocolate ice cream over sauce.

4. Top with alternating scoops of vanilla and chocolate ice cream. Cover; return to freezer until serving time. Drizzle with additional syrup just before serving. ■

chocolate marbled peanut butter pie

MAKES 6 TO 8 SERVINGS

½ cup REESE'S Creamy Peanut Butter

1 package (3 ounces) cream cheese, softened

½ teaspoon vanilla extract

1 cup powdered sugar

½ cup milk

1 tub (8 ounces) frozen non-dairy whipped topping, thawed

1 extra serving-size packaged graham crumb crust (9 ounce)

½ cup HERSHEY'S SPECIAL DARK Chocolate Chips or HERSHEY'S Semi-Sweet Chocolate Chips

1. Beat peanut butter, cream cheese and vanilla in medium bowl on medium speed of mixer until smooth. Gradually add powdered sugar and milk, beating until smooth. Fold in whipped topping. Place 1 cup peanut butter mixture in separate bowl. Spread remaining mixture in crust.

2. Place chocolate chips in small microwave-safe bowl. Microwave at MEDIUM (50%) 30 seconds or until chocolate is melted and smooth when stirred. Stir chocolate into reserved peanut butter mixture, blending thoroughly; drop by tablespoons onto top of pie. Using knife or spatula, gently swirl for marbled effect.

3. Cover; freeze 4 to 5 hours or until firm. Garnish as desired. ■

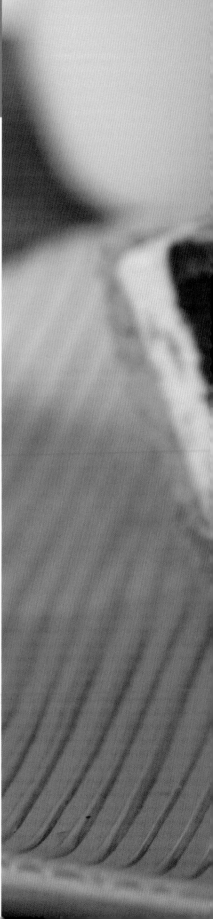

chocolate magic mousse pie

MAKES 6 TO 8 SERVINGS

1 envelope unflavored gelatin

2 tablespoons cold water

¼ cup boiling water

1 cup sugar

½ cup HERSHEY'S Cocoa

2 cups (1 pint) cold whipping cream

2 teaspoons vanilla extract

1 packaged graham cracker crumb crust (6 ounces)

Refrigerated light whipped cream in pressurized can or frozen non-dairy whipped topping, thawed

HERSHEY'S MINI KISSES BRAND Milk Chocolates

1. Sprinkle gelatin over cold water in small bowl; let stand 2 minutes to soften. Add boiling water; stir until gelatin is completely dissolved and mixture is clear. Cool slightly.

2. Mix sugar and cocoa in large bowl; add whipping cream and vanilla. Beat on medium speed, scraping bottom of bowl often, until mixture is stiff. Pour in gelatin mixture; beat until well blended.

3. Spoon into crust. Refrigerate about 3 hours. Garnish with whipped cream and chocolates. ■

upside-down hot fudge sundae pie

⅔ cup butter or margarine

⅓ cup HERSHEY'S Cocoa

2 eggs

¼ cup milk

1 teaspoon vanilla extract

1 cup packed light brown sugar

½ cup granulated sugar

1 tablespoon all-purpose flour

⅛ teaspoon salt

1 unbaked (9-inch) pie crust

2 bananas, peeled and thinly sliced

Ice cream, any flavor

Whipped topping

1. Heat oven to 350°F.

2. Melt butter in medium saucepan over low heat. Add cocoa; stir until smooth. Remove from heat. Stir together eggs, milk and vanilla in small bowl. Add egg mixture to cocoa mixture; stir with whisk until smooth and slightly thickened. Add brown sugar, granulated sugar, flour and salt; stir with whisk until smooth. Pour mixture into unbaked crust.

3. Bake 30 to 35 minutes until edge is set. (Center will be soft.) Cool about 2 hours. Just before serving, top each serving with banana slices, ice cream and whipped topping. ■

classic boston cream pie

⅓ cup shortening

1 cup sugar

2 eggs

1 teaspoon vanilla extract

1¼ cups all-purpose flour

1½ teaspoons baking powder

¼ teaspoon salt

¾ cup milk

RICH FILLING
(recipe follows)

DARK COCOA GLAZE
(recipe follows)

1. Heat oven to 350°F. Grease and flour 9-inch round baking pan.

2. Beat shortening, sugar, eggs and vanilla in large bowl until fluffy. Stir together flour, baking powder and salt; add alternately with milk to shortening mixture, beating well after each addition. Pour batter into prepared pan.

3. Bake 30 to 35 minutes or until wooden pick inserted in center comes out clean. Cool 10 minutes; remove from pan to wire rack. Cool completely.

4. Prepare RICH FILLING. With long serrated knife, cut cake in half horizontally. Place one layer, cut side up, on serving plate; spread with prepared filling. Top with remaining layer, cut side down. Prepare DARK COCOA GLAZE; spread over cake, allowing glaze to run down sides. Refrigerate several hours or until cold. Garnish as desired. Refrigerate leftover pie.

RICH FILLING

⅓ cup sugar

2 tablespoons cornstarch

1½ cups milk

2 egg yolks, slightly beaten

1 tablespoon butter or margarine

1 teaspoon vanilla extract

Stir together sugar and cornstarch in medium saucepan; gradually add milk and egg yolks, stirring until blended. Cook over medium heat, stirring constantly, until mixture comes to a boil. Boil 1 minute, stirring constantly. Remove from heat; stir in butter and vanilla. Cover; refrigerate several hours or until cold.

DARK COCOA GLAZE

3 tablespoons water

2 tablespoons butter or margarine

3 tablespoons HERSHEY'S Cocoa

1 cup powdered sugar

½ teaspoon vanilla extract

Heat water and butter in small saucepan over medium heat until mixture comes to a boil; remove from heat. Immediately stir in cocoa. Gradually add powdered sugar and vanilla, beating with whisk until smooth and of desired consistency; cool slightly. ∎

fudgey mocha nut pie

MAKES 8 SERVINGS

6 tablespoons butter or margarine

⅓ cup HERSHEY'S Cocoa

1 can (14 ounces) sweetened
condensed milk
(not evaporated milk)

⅓ cup water

2 eggs, beaten

2 to 3 tablespoons powdered
instant coffee

1 cup HERSHEY'S SPECIAL DARK
Chocolate Chips or HERSHEY'S
Semi-Sweet Chocolate Chips

1 cup coarsely chopped pecans

1 teaspoon vanilla extract

1 unbaked 9-inch pie crust

Sweetened whipped
cream (optional)

1. Heat oven to 350°F.

2. Melt butter in medium saucepan over low heat. Add cocoa; stir until smooth. Stir in sweetened condensed milk, water, eggs, instant coffee and chocolate chips; whisk constantly until well blended and chocolate is melted. Remove from heat.

3. Stir in pecans and vanilla. Pour into unbaked pie crust.

4. Bake 40 minutes or until center is set. (Center will still appear moist.) Cool completely. Garnish with sweetened whipped cream, if desired. Cover; refrigerate leftover pie. ■

easy chocolate coconut cream pie

MAKES 8 SERVINGS

1 unbaked (9-inch) pie crust

1 package (4-serving size) vanilla cook and serve pudding and pie filling mix*

½ cup sugar

¼ cup HERSHEY'S Cocoa or HERSHEY'S SPECIAL DARK Cocoa

1¾ cups milk

1 cup MOUNDS Sweetened Coconut Flakes

2 cups frozen non-dairy whipped topping, thawed

*Do not use instant pudding mix.

1. Bake pie crust; cool completely.

2. Stir together dry pudding mix, sugar and cocoa in large microwave-safe bowl. Gradually add milk, stirring with whisk until blended.

3. Microwave at HIGH (100%) 6 minutes, stirring with whisk every 2 minutes, until mixture boils and is thickened and smooth. If necessary, microwave an additional 1 minute; stir.

4. Cool 5 minutes in bowl; stir in coconut. Pour into prepared pie crust. Carefully press plastic wrap directly onto pie filling. Cool; refrigerate 6 hours or until firm. Top with whipped topping. Garnish as desired. ■

mini chocolate pies

1 package (4-serving size) vanilla cook & serve pudding and pie filling mix*

1 cup HERSHEY'S Mini Chips Semi-Sweet Chocolate

1 package (4 ounces) single-serve graham cracker crusts (6 crusts)

Whipped topping

Additional HERSHEY'S Mini Chips Semi-Sweet Chocolate or HERSHEY'S Semi-Sweet Chocolate chips (optional)

*Do not use instant pudding mix.

1. Prepare pudding and pie filling mix as directed on package; remove from heat. Immediately add 1 cup small chocolate chips; stir until melted. Cool 5 minutes, stirring occasionally.

2. Pour filling into crusts; press plastic wrap directly onto surface. Refrigerate several hours or until firm. Garnish with whipped topping and small chocolate chips. ■

REESE'S peanut butter & HERSHEY'S KISSES pie

MAKES 8 SERVINGS

About 42 HERSHEY'S KISSES BRAND Milk Chocolates, divided

2 tablespoons milk

1 packaged (8-inch) crumb crust (6 ounces)

1 package (8 ounces) cream cheese, softened

¾ cup sugar

1 cup REESE'S Creamy Peanut Butter

1 tub (8 ounces) frozen non-dairy whipped topping, thawed and divided

1. Remove wrappers from chocolates. Place 26 chocolates and milk in small microwave-safe bowl. Microwave at MEDIUM (50%) 1 minute or just until melted and smooth when stirred. Spread evenly on bottom of crust. Refrigerate about 30 minutes.

2. Beat cream cheese with electric mixer on medium speed in medium bowl until smooth; gradually beat in sugar, then peanut butter, beating well after each addition. Reserve ½ cup whipped topping; fold remaining whipped topping into peanut butter mixture. Spoon into crust over chocolate. Cover; refrigerate about 6 hours or until set.

3. Garnish with reserved whipped topping and remaining chocolates. Cover; refrigerate leftover pie. ■

easy chocolate cheesepie

MAKES 6 TO 8 SERVINGS

4 sections (½ ounce each) HERSHEY'S Unsweetened Chocolate Premium Baking Bar, broken into pieces

¼ cup (½ stick) butter or margarine, softened

¾ cup sugar

1 package (3 ounces) cream cheese, softened

1 teaspoon milk

2 cups frozen whipped non-dairy topping, thawed

1 packaged crumb crust (6 ounces)

Additional whipped topping (optional)

Chocolate curls can jazz up any dessert—they're an easy way to add a dramatic finish.

1. Place chocolate in small microwave-safe bowl. Microwave at MEDIUM (50%) 1 to 1½ minutes or until chocolate is melted and smooth when stirred.

2. Beat butter, sugar, cream cheese and milk in medium bowl until well blended and smooth; fold in melted chocolate.

3. Fold in 2 cups whipped topping; spoon into crust. Cover; refrigerate until firm, about 3 hours. Garnish with additional whipped topping, if desired. ■

HERSHEY'S cocoa cream pie

1 baked (9-inch) pie crust or graham cracker crumb crust, cooled

1¼ cups sugar

½ cup HERSHEY'S Cocoa

⅓ cup cornstarch

¼ teaspoon salt

3 cups milk

3 tablespoons butter or margarine

1½ teaspoons vanilla extract

Sweetened whipped cream

1. Prepare crust; cool.

2. Stir together sugar, cocoa, cornstarch and salt in medium saucepan. Gradually add milk, stirring until smooth. Cook over medium heat, stirring constantly, until mixture comes to a boil; boil 1 minute.

3. Remove from heat; stir in butter and vanilla. Pour into prepared crust. Press plastic wrap directly onto surface. Cool to room temperature. Refrigerate 6 to 8 hours. Serve with sweetened whipped cream. Garnish as desired. Cover; refrigerate leftover pie. ■

TIMELESS
TREATS &
DESSERTS

Blissful Delights

chocolate mini-puffs

MAKES ABOUT 2 TO 2½ DOZEN MINI-PUFFS

½ cup water

¼ cup (½ stick) butter or margarine

⅛ teaspoon salt

½ cup all-purpose flour

2 eggs

CHOCOLATE MOUSSE FILLING
(recipe follows)

Powdered sugar or
CHOCOLATE GLAZE
(recipe follows)

1. Heat oven to 400°F.

2. Combine water, butter and salt in medium saucepan. Cook over medium heat, stirring constantly, until mixture comes to full rolling boil; turn heat to low.

3. Add flour all at once; cook over low heat, stirring vigorously, until mixture leaves side of pan and forms a ball, about 1 minute. Remove from heat; cool slightly. Add eggs, one at a time, beating with wooden spoon until smooth and velvety. Drop by scant teaspoonfuls onto ungreased cookie sheet.

4. Bake 25 to 30 minutes or until puffed and golden brown. Remove from oven; cool on wire rack.

5. Prepare CHOCOLATE MOUSSE FILLING. Slice off tops of puffs. With spoon, fill puffs with filling or pipe filling into puffs using a pastry bag fitted with ¼-inch tip. Replace tops and sprinkle with powdered sugar or prepare CHOCOLATE GLAZE; drizzle onto puffs. Refrigerate until serving time. Cover; refrigerate leftover puffs.

CHOCOLATE MOUSSE FILLING

1 teaspoon unflavored gelatin

1 tablespoon cold water

2 tablespoons boiling water

½ cup sugar

¼ cup HERSHEY'S Cocoa

1 cup (½ pint) cold whipping cream

1 teaspoon vanilla extract

1. Sprinkle gelatin over cold water in small bowl; let stand 1 minute to soften. Add boiling water; stir until gelatin is completely dissolved and mixture is clear. Cool slightly.

2. Stir together sugar and cocoa in medium bowl; add whipping cream and vanilla. Beat at medium speed, scraping bottom of bowl occasionally, until stiff; pour in gelatin mixture and beat until well blended. Refrigerate 30 minutes.

MAKES ABOUT 2 CUPS FILLING

CHOCOLATE GLAZE

1. Melt 2 tablespoons butter or margarine in small saucepan over low heat; add 2 tablespoons HERSHEY'S Cocoa and 2 tablespoons water. Cook and stir over low heat until smooth and slightly thickened; do not boil. Remove from heat; cool slightly.

2. Gradually add in 1 cup powdered sugar and ½ teaspoon vanilla extract, beating to desired consistency.

MAKES ABOUT ¾ CUP GLAZE ■

chocolate cups with lemon cream

½ cup sugar

¼ cup plus 2 tablespoons all-purpose flour

2 tablespoons HERSHEY'S Cocoa

2 egg whites

¼ cup (½ stick) butter or margarine, melted

CHOCOLATE COATING (recipe follows)

LEMON CREAM (recipe follows)

Freshly shredded lemon peel (optional)

1. Heat oven to 400°F. Grease and flour cookie sheet.

2. Stir together sugar, flour and cocoa in small bowl. Add egg whites and butter; beat until smooth. Drop teaspoonfuls of mixture onto prepared baking sheet; with back of spoon, spread thinly into 5-inch circles.

3. Bake 6 to 7 minutes or until set. Immediately remove from cookie sheet; place, top side down, on inverted juice glasses. Mold to form wavy edges. (If chocolate cracks, gently press together with fingers.)

Let stand about 30 minutes or until hard and completely cool.

4. Prepare CHOCOLATE COATING. With small brush, coat inside of cups with prepared coating. Refrigerate 20 minutes or until coating is set.

5. Meanwhile, prepare LEMON CREAM; spoon scant ½ cup LEMON CREAM into each cup. Garnish with shredded lemon peel, if desired. Cover; refrigerate leftover desserts.

Lemon and orange zest come from the outermost rind of the fruit. Use it to add a strong citrus flavor to food.

CHOCOLATE COATING

¾ cup HERSHEY'S SPECIAL DARK Chocolate Chips or HERSHEY'S Semi-Sweet Chocolate Chips

1 teaspoon shortening (do not use butter, margarine, spread or oil)

Place chocolate chips and shortening in small microwave-safe bowl. Microwave at MEDIUM (50%) 45 seconds; stir. If necessary, microwave at MEDIUM an additional 15 seconds at a time, stirring after each heating, just until chips are melted when stirred.

LEMON CREAM

1 package (4-serving size) instant lemon pudding and pie filling mix

1 cup milk

⅛ teaspoon lemon extract

1½ cups frozen non-dairy whipped topping, thawed

Combine pudding mix, milk and lemon extract in small bowl. Beat on low speed 2 minutes. Fold in whipped topping; refrigerate 30 minutes or until set.

MAKES ABOUT 2½ CUPS CREAM ■

cherry-glazed chocolate torte

MAKES 10 TO 12 SERVINGS

½ cup (1 stick) butter or margarine, melted

1 cup granulated sugar

1 teaspoon vanilla extract

2 eggs

½ cup all-purpose flour

⅓ cup HERSHEY'S Cocoa

¼ teaspoon baking powder

¼ teaspoon salt

1 package (8 ounces) cream cheese, softened

1 cup powdered sugar

1 cup frozen non-dairy whipped topping, thawed

1 can (21 ounces) cherry pie filling, divided

1. Heat oven to 350°F. Grease bottom of 9-inch springform pan.

2. Stir together butter, granulated sugar and vanilla in large bowl. Add eggs; using spoon, beat well. Stir together flour, cocoa, baking powder and salt; gradually add to egg mixture, beating until well blended. Spread batter in prepared pan.

3. Bake 25 to 30 minutes or until cake is set. (Cake will be fudgey and will not test done.) Remove from oven; cool completely in pan on wire rack.

4. Beat cream cheese and powdered sugar in medium bowl until well blended; gradually fold in whipped topping, blending well. Spread over top of cake. Spread 1 cup cherry pie filling over cream layer; refrigerate several hours. With knife, loosen cake from side of pan; remove side of pan. Cut into wedges; garnish with remaining pie filling. Cover; refrigerate leftover dessert. ■

milk chocolate pots de crème

2 cups (11.5-ounce package) HERSHEY'S Milk Chocolate Chips

½ cup light cream

½ teaspoon vanilla extract

Sweetened whipped cream (optional)

1. Place milk chocolate chips and light cream in medium microwave-safe bowl. Microwave at MEDIUM (50%) 1 minute; stir. If necessary, microwave at MEDIUM an additional 15 seconds at a time, stirring after each heating, just until chocolate is melted and smooth when stirred. Stir in vanilla.

2. Pour into demitasse cups or very small dessert dishes. Cover; refrigerate until firm. Serve cold with sweetened whipped cream, if desired. ■

chocolate syrup swirl dessert

MAKES 10 TO 12 SERVINGS

CRUMB CRUST
(recipe follows)

1 envelope unflavored gelatin

¼ cup cold water

1 package (8 ounces) cream cheese, softened

¼ cup sugar

1 teaspoon vanilla extract

¾ cup HERSHEY'S Syrup, chilled

¾ cup milk

VANILLA FILLING
(recipe follows)

Additional HERSHEY'S Syrup
(optional)

1. Prepare CRUMB CRUST.

2. Sprinkle gelatin over water in small saucepan; let stand 2 minutes. Cook over low heat, stirring constantly, until gelatin is dissolved.

3. Beat cream cheese, sugar and vanilla in large bowl until creamy. Add syrup, gelatin mixture and milk; blend well. Refrigerate, stirring occasionally, until mixture mounds from spoon, about 20 minutes.

4. Spoon half of chocolate mixture into prepared crust; top with half of VANILLA FILLING. Repeat procedure, ending with spoonfuls of VANILLA FILLING on top. Using knife or metal spatula, gently swirl through dessert. Cover; refrigerate several hours until set. Serve with additional syrup, if desired.

CRUMB CRUST

Stir together 2 cups vanilla wafer crumbs (about 60 wafers) and ⅓ cup melted butter or margarine in medium bowl. Press mixture onto bottom and 1½ inches up side of 9-inch springform pan or 10-inch pie plate. Refrigerate about 30 minutes or until firm.

VANILLA FILLING

1 teaspoon unflavored gelatin

1 tablespoon cold water

2 tablespoons boiling water

1 cup (½ pint) cold whipping cream

2 tablespoons sugar

½ teaspoon vanilla extract

Sprinkle gelatin over cold water in small cup; let stand 1 minute. Add boiling water; stir until gelatin is completely dissolved; cool slightly. Combine whipping cream, sugar and vanilla in medium bowl; beat until slightly thickened. Gradually add gelatin mixture; beat until stiff. ■

viennese chocolate torte

¼ cup HERSHEY'S Cocoa

¼ cup boiling water

⅓ cup shortening

¾ cup sugar

½ teaspoon vanilla extract

1 egg

1 cup all-purpose flour

¾ teaspoon baking soda

¼ teaspoon salt

⅔ cup buttermilk or sour milk*

¼ cup seedless black raspberry preserves

CREAM FILLING
(recipe follows)

COCOA GLAZE
(recipe follows)

MOUNDS Coconut Flakes, toasted

*To sour milk: Use 2 teaspoons white vinegar plus milk to equal ⅔ cup.

1. Heat oven to 350°F. Lightly grease 15½×10½×1-inch jelly-roll pan; line pan with wax paper and lightly grease paper.

2. Stir together cocoa and boiling water in small bowl until smooth; set aside. Beat shortening, sugar and vanilla in medium bowl until creamy; beat in egg. Stir together flour, baking soda and salt; add alternately with buttermilk to shortening mixture. Add reserved cocoa mixture, beating just until blended. Spread batter in pan.

3. Bake 16 to 18 minutes or until wooden pick inserted in center comes out clean. Cool 10 minutes; remove from pan. Remove wax paper; cool completely. Cut cake crosswise into three equal pieces. Place one piece on serving plate; spread 2 tablespoons preserves evenly on top of cake. Spread half of CREAM FILLING over preserves. Repeat layering. Glaze top of torte with COCOA GLAZE, allowing some to drizzle down sides. Garnish with coconut. Refrigerate several hours. Cover; refrigerate leftover torte.

CREAM FILLING

Beat 1 cup whipping cream, 2 tablespoons powdered sugar and 1 teaspoon vanilla extract in small bowl until stiff.

MAKES ABOUT 2 CUPS FILLING

COCOA GLAZE

2 tablespoons butter or margarine

2 tablespoons HERSHEY'S Cocoa

2 tablespoons water

1 cup powdered sugar

½ teaspoon vanilla extract

Melt butter in saucepan. Stir in cocoa and water. Cook, stirring constantly, until mixture thickens. Do not boil. Remove from heat. Whisk in powdered sugar gradually. Add vanilla and beat with whisk until smooth. Add additional water ½ teaspoon at a time until desired consistency. ■

peanut butter fondue

MAKES ABOUT 3 CUPS FONDUE

Selection of fruits and other fondue dippers

3⅓ cups, 2 (10-ounce packages), REESE'S Peanut Butter Chips

1½ cups light cream

1. Prepare ahead of time a selection of fresh fruit chunks for dipping: apples, bananas, pears, peaches, cherries, pineapple, oranges (brush fresh fruit with lemon juice to prevent browning). Cover; refrigerate until ready to serve. (Dried apples and apricots, marshmallows and bite-size pieces of pound cake can also be used for dipping.)

2. Place peanut butter chips and light cream in medium microwave-safe bowl. Microwave at MEDIUM (50%) 1½ minutes; stir. If necessary, microwave at MEDIUM an additional 30 seconds at a time, stirring after each heating, until chips are melted and mixture is smooth when stirred.

3. Pour into fondue pot; keep warm over low heat. Dip chunks of fruit into warm sauce with forks. Keep leftover sauce covered and refrigerated.

NOTE

Recipe may be halved using 1 package (10 ounces) REESE'S Peanut Butter Chips and ¾ cup light cream. ■

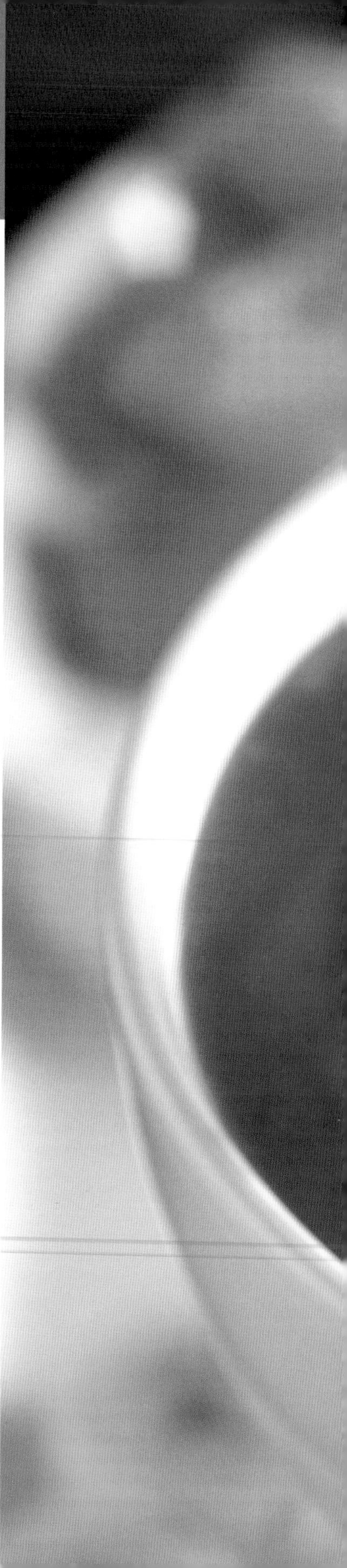

deep dark mousse

MAKES 4 TO 6 SERVINGS

¼ cup sugar

1 teaspoon unflavored gelatin

½ cup milk

1 cup HERSHEY'S SPECIAL DARK
Chocolate Chips

2 teaspoons vanilla extract

1 cup (½ pint) cold whipping cream

Sweetened whipped
cream (optional)

1. Stir together sugar and gelatin in small saucepan; stir in milk. Let stand 2 minutes to soften gelatin. Cook over medium heat, stirring constantly, until mixture just begins to boil.

2. Remove from heat. Immediately add chocolate chips; stir until melted. Stir in vanilla; cool to room temperature.

3. Beat whipping cream with electric mixer on medium speed in large bowl until stiff peaks form. Add half of chocolate mixture and gently fold until nearly combined; add remaining chocolate mixture and fold just until blended. Spoon into serving dish or individual dishes. Refrigerate. Garnish with sweetened whipped cream, if desired, just before serving. ■

hot chocolate soufflé

MAKES 8 TO 10 SERVINGS

1 cup HERSHEY'S Cocoa

1¼ cups sugar, divided

½ cup all-purpose flour

¼ teaspoon salt

2 cups milk

6 egg yolks, well beaten

2 tablespoons butter or margarine

1 teaspoon vanilla extract

8 egg whites

¼ teaspoon cream of tartar

Sweetened whipped cream

1. Move oven rack to lowest position. Heat oven to 350°F. Lightly butter 2½-quart soufflé dish; sprinkle with sugar. For collar, cut a length of heavy-duty aluminum foil to fit around soufflé dish; fold in thirds lengthwise. Lightly butter one side of foil. Attach foil, buttered side in, around outside of dish, allowing foil to extend at least 2 inches above dish. Secure foil with tape or string.

2. Stir together cocoa, 1 cup sugar, flour and salt in large saucepan; gradually stir in milk. Cook over medium heat, stirring constantly with wire whisk, until mixture boils; remove from heat. Gradually stir small amount of chocolate mixture into beaten egg yolks; blend well. Add egg mixture to chocolate mixture in pan, blending well. Cook and stir 1 minute. Add butter and vanilla, stirring until blended. Set aside; cool 20 minutes.

3. Beat egg whites with cream of tartar in large bowl until soft peaks form; gradually add remaining ¼ cup sugar, beating until stiff peaks form. Gently fold about one-third of beaten egg white mixture into chocolate mixture. Lightly fold chocolate mixture, one half at a time, into remaining beaten egg white mixture just until blended; do not overfold.

4. Gently pour mixture into prepared dish; smooth top with spatula. Gently place dish in larger baking pan; pour hot water into larger pan to depth of 1 inch.

5. Bake 1 hour and 5 to 10 minutes or until puffed and set. Remove soufflé dish from water. Carefully remove foil. Serve immediately with sweetened whipped cream. ■

HERSHEY'S white and dark chocolate fudge torte

MAKES 10 TO 12 SERVINGS

1 cup (2 sticks) butter or margarine, melted

1½ cups sugar

1 teaspoon vanilla extract

3 eggs, separated

⅔ cup HERSHEY'S Cocoa

½ cup all-purpose flour

3 tablespoons water

2 cups (12-ounce package) HERSHEY'S Premier White Chips, divided

⅛ teaspoon cream of tartar

SATINY GLAZE
(recipe follows)

WHITE DECORATOR DRIZZLE
(recipe follows)

1. Heat oven to 350°F. Line bottom of 9-inch springform pan with foil; grease foil and side of pan.

2. Combine butter, sugar and vanilla in large bowl; beat well. Add egg yolks, one at a time, beating well after each addition. Blend in cocoa, flour and water. Stir in 1⅔ cups white chips. Reserve remaining chips for drizzle. Beat egg whites with cream of tartar in small bowl until stiff peaks form; fold into chocolate mixture. Pour batter into prepared pan.

3. Bake 45 minutes or until top begins to crack slightly. (Cake will not test done in center.) Cool 1 hour. Cover; refrigerate until firm. Remove side of pan. Prepare SATINY GLAZE and WHITE DECORATOR DRIZZLE. Pour prepared glaze over torte; spread evenly over top and side. Decorate top of torte with prepared drizzle.* Cover; refrigerate until serving time. Refrigerate leftover torte.

*To decorate, drizzle with spoon or place in pastry bag with writing tip.

SATINY GLAZE

1 cup HERSHEY'S SPECIAL DARK Chocolate Chips or HERSHEY'S Semi-Sweet Chocolate Chips

¼ cup whipping cream

Place chocolate chips and whipping cream in small microwave-safe bowl. Microwave at MEDIUM (50%) 1 minute; stir. If necessary, microwave at MEDIUM an additional 15 seconds at a time, stirring after each heating, just until chips are melted when stirred. Cool until lukewarm and slightly thickened.

MAKES ABOUT ¾ CUP GLAZE

WHITE DECORATOR DRIZZLE

⅓ cup HERSHEY'S Premier White Chips (reserved from torte)

2 teaspoons shortening (do not use butter, margarine, spread or oil)

Place white chips and shortening in small microwave-safe bowl. Microwave at MEDIUM (50%) 20 to 30 seconds; stir. If necessary, microwave at MEDIUM an additional 15 seconds at a time, stirring after each heating, just until chips are melted when stirred. ■

easy chocoberry cream dessert

2 packages (3 ounces each) ladyfingers, split

1 package (10 ounces) frozen strawberries in syrup, thawed and drained

2 envelopes unflavored gelatin

2 cups milk, divided

1 cup sugar

⅓ cup HERSHEY'S Cocoa or HERSHEY'S SPECIAL DARK Cocoa

¼ cup (½ stick) butter or margarine

1 teaspoon vanilla extract

2 cups frozen non-dairy whipped topping, thawed

Additional whipped topping (optional)

Fresh strawberries (optional)

Mint leaves (optional)

1. Place ladyfingers, cut side in, on bottom and around sides of 9-inch springform pan.

2. Purée strawberries in food processor. Sprinkle gelatin over 1 cup milk in medium saucepan; let stand 2 minutes to soften. Add sugar, cocoa and butter. Cook over medium heat, stirring constantly, until mixture is hot and gelatin is completely dissolved. Remove from heat; stir in remaining 1 cup milk, vanilla and puréed strawberries. Refrigerate until mixture begins to thicken.

3. Fold 2 cups whipped topping into gelatin mixture. Pour mixture into prepared pan. Cover; refrigerate until mixture is firm. Just before serving, remove side of pan. Garnish with additional whipped topping, fresh strawberries and mint, if desired. Cover; refrigerate leftover dessert. ■

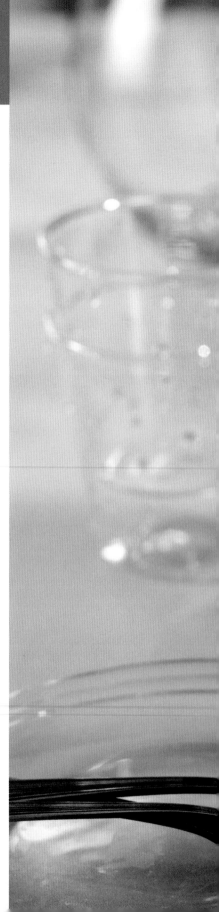

chocolate raspberry dessert

MAKES ABOUT 12 SERVINGS

1 cup all-purpose flour

1 cup sugar

½ cup (1 stick) butter or margarine, softened

¼ teaspoon baking powder

4 eggs

1½ cups (16-ounce can) HERSHEY'S Syrup

RASPBERRY CREAM CENTER (recipe follows)

CHOCOLATE GLAZE (recipe follows)

1. Heat oven to 350°F. Grease 13×9×2-inch baking pan.

2. Combine flour, sugar, butter, baking powder and eggs in large bowl; beat until smooth. Add syrup; blend thoroughly. Pour batter into prepared pan.

3. Bake 25 to 30 minutes or until wooden pick inserted in center comes out clean. Cool completely in pan on wire rack. Spread RASPBERRY CREAM CENTER on cake. Cover; refrigerate. Pour CHOCOLATE GLAZE over chilled dessert. Cover; refrigerate at least 1 hour before serving. Cover; refrigerate leftover dessert.

RASPBERRY CREAM CENTER

Combine 2 cups powdered sugar, ½ cup (1 stick) softened butter or margarine and 2 tablespoons raspberry-flavored liqueur* in small bowl; beat until smooth. (A few drops red food coloring may be added, if desired.)

*¼ cup raspberry preserves mixed with 1 teaspoon water may be substituted for the raspberry-flavored liqueur.

CHOCOLATE GLAZE

Melt 6 tablespoons butter or margarine and 1 cup HERSHEY'S SPECIAL DARK Chocolate Chips or HERSHEY'S Semi-Sweet Chocolate Chips in small saucepan over very low heat. Remove from heat; stir until smooth. Cool slightly. ■

flourless chocolate torte

1¼ cups (2½ sticks) butter

¾ cup HERSHEY'S Cocoa

2 cups sugar, divided

6 eggs, separated

¼ cup water

1 teaspoon vanilla extract

1 cup blanched sliced almonds, toasted and ground*

½ cup plain dry bread crumbs

MOCHA CREAM (recipe follows)

Additional HERSHEY'S Cocoa, for garnish

*To toast almonds: Heat oven to 350°F. Place almonds in single layer in shallow baking pan. Bake 7 to 8 minutes, stirring occasionally, until light brown. Cool.

1. Heat oven to 350°F. Grease and flour 9-inch springform pan. Melt butter in saucepan over low heat. Add cocoa and 1½ cups sugar; stir until smooth. Cool to room temperature.

2. Beat egg yolks in large bowl until thick. Gradually beat in chocolate mixture; stir in water and vanilla. Combine ground almonds and bread crumbs; stir into chocolate mixture.

3. Beat egg whites until foamy; gradually add remaining ½ cup sugar, beating until soft peaks form. Fold about one-third of egg whites into chocolate. Fold chocolate into remaining egg whites. Pour into prepared pan.

4. Bake 50 to 60 minutes or until wooden pick inserted in center comes out clean. Cool 10 minutes. Loosen cake from side of pan; remove pan. Cool completely. Spread MOCHA CREAM over top. Sift with cocoa just before serving. Store covered in refrigerator.

MOCHA CREAM

Combine 1 cup (½ pint) cold whipping cream, 2 tablespoons powdered sugar, 1½ teaspoons powdered instant coffee granules dissolved in 1 teaspoon water, and ½ teaspoon vanilla extract in medium bowl; beat until stiff.

MAKES ABOUT 2 CUPS ■

chocolate dream cups

MAKES 6 DESSERT CUPS

1 cup HERSHEY'S SPECIAL DARK Chocolate Chips or HERSHEY'S Semi-Sweet Chocolate Chips

1 teaspoon shortening (do not use butter, margarine, spread or oil)

CHOCOLATE FILLING or RASPBERRY FILLING (recipes follow)

1. Line 6 muffin cups (2½ inches in diameter) with paper cup liners.

2. Place chocolate chips and shortening in small microwave-safe bowl. Microwave at MEDIUM (50%) 1 minute; stir. If necessary, microwave at MEDIUM an additional 30 seconds or until chips are melted and mixture is smooth when stirred.

3. Coat inside pleated surface and bottoms of cup liners thickly and evenly with melted chocolate using a soft-bristled pastry brush. Refrigerate coated cups 10 minutes or until set; recoat any thin spots with melted chocolate. (If necessary, chocolate can be reheated on MEDIUM a few seconds.) Refrigerate cups until very firm, 2 hours or overnight. Carefully peel paper from each chocolate cup. Cover; refrigerate until ready to use.

4. Prepare either CHOCOLATE FILLING or RASPBERRY FILLING. Spoon or pipe into chocolate cups; refrigerate until set. Garnish as desired.

CHOCOLATE FILLING

1 teaspoon unflavored gelatin

1 tablespoon cold water

2 tablespoons boiling water

½ cup sugar

¼ cup HERSHEY'S Cocoa

1 cup (8 ounces) cold whipping cream

1 teaspoon vanilla extract

1. Sprinkle gelatin over cold water in small bowl; let stand 1 minute to soften. Add boiling water; stir until gelatin is completely dissolved and mixture is clear. Cool slightly.

2. Stir together sugar and cocoa in another small bowl; add whipping cream and vanilla. Beat on medium speed, scraping bottom of bowl occasionally until stiff. Pour in gelatin mixture; beat until well blended.

RASPBERRY FILLING

1 package (10 ounces) frozen red raspberries, thawed

1 teaspoon unflavored gelatin

1 tablespoon cold water

2 tablespoons boiling water

1 cup (8 ounces) cold whipping cream

¼ cup powdered sugar

½ teaspoon vanilla extract

3 to 4 drops red food coloring

1. Drain raspberries; press berries through sieve to remove seeds. Discard seeds.

2. Sprinkle gelatin over cold water in small bowl; let stand 1 minute to soften. Add boiling water; stir until gelatin is completely dissolved and mixture is clear. Cool slightly.

3. Beat whipping cream, sugar and vanilla in another small bowl until soft peaks form; pour in gelatin mixture and beat until stiff. Carefully fold in raspberry purée and food coloring; refrigerate 20 minutes. ■

HUGS & KISSES crescents

MAKES 8 CRESCENTS

1 package (8 ounces) refrigerated crescent dinner rolls

24 HERSHEY'S KISSES BRAND Milk Chocolates or HERSHEY'S HUGS BRAND Candies

Powdered sugar

1. Heat oven to 375°F. Separate dough into 8 triangles. Remove wrappers from chocolates.

2. Place 2 chocolates at center of wide end of each triangle; place an additional chocolate on top of other two pieces. Starting at wide end, roll to opposite point; pinch edges to seal. Place rolls, pointed side down, on ungreased cookie sheet. Curve into crescent shape.

3. Bake 10 minutes or until lightly browned. Cool slightly; sift with powdered sugar. Serve warm.

NOTE

Leftover crescents can be reheated in microwave for a few seconds. ■

pears with chocolate-orange sauce

MAKES 6 SERVINGS

6 fresh pears

1½ cups apple juice

1 teaspoon vanilla extract

CHOCOLATE-ORANGE SAUCE
(recipe follows)

1. Slice piece off bottom of pears to make a flat base. Peel pears and core from bottom but leave stems intact.

2. Combine juice with vanilla in large saucepan; add pears, base side down. Heat to boiling; reduce heat. Cover; simmer, spooning juice over pears occasionally, 20 to 25 minutes or until pears are tender.

3. Meanwhile, prepare CHOCOLATE-ORANGE SAUCE. To serve, place pear base side down in serving dish; spoon about 1 tablespoon warm sauce over top.

CHOCOLATE-ORANGE SAUCE

¾ cup HERSHEY'S SPECIAL DARK Chocolate Chips or HERSHEY'S Semi-Sweet Chocolate Chips

1 tablespoon shortening (do not use butter, margarine, spread or oil)

¼ teaspoon orange extract

Place all ingredients in medium microwave-safe bowl. Microwave at MEDIUM (50%) 30 seconds; stir. If necessary, microwave at MEDIUM an additional 10 seconds at a time, stirring after each heating, until chocolate is melted and mixture is smooth when stirred. Serve warm sauce over hot poached pears. ■

SPECIAL DARK fudge fondue

MAKES 1 1/2 CUPS

2 cups (12-ounce package) HERSHEY'S SPECIAL DARK Chocolate Chips

1/2 cup light cream

2 teaspoons vanilla extract

Assorted fondue dippers such as marshmallows, cherries, grapes, mandarin orange segments, pineapple chunks, strawberries, slices of other fresh fruits, small pieces of cake or small brownies

1. Place chocolate chips and light cream in medium microwave-safe bowl. Microwave at MEDIUM (50%) 1 minute or just until chips are melted and mixture is smooth when stirred. Stir in vanilla.

2. Pour into fondue pot or chafing dish; serve warm with fondue dippers. If mixture thickens, stir in additional light cream, 1 tablespoon at a time. Refrigerate leftover fondue.

STOVETOP DIRECTIONS

Combine chocolate chips and light cream in heavy medium saucepan. Cook over low heat, stirring constantly, until chips are melted and mixture is hot. Stir in vanilla and continue as in Step 2 above. ■

mocha brownie nut torte

1 cup (2 sticks) butter

1 package (4 ounces) HERSHEY'S Unsweetened Chocolate Premium Baking Bar, broken into pieces

4 eggs

1 teaspoon vanilla extract

2 cups granulated sugar

1 cup all-purpose flour

1 cup finely chopped pecans

1 package (8 ounces) cream cheese, softened

1 cup powdered sugar

½ cup chilled whipping cream

2 to 3 teaspoons powdered instant coffee

CHOCOLATE GLAZE (recipe follows)

1. Heat oven to 350°F. Line bottom and sides of 9-inch round cake pan with foil, extending foil beyond sides. Grease foil.

2. Place butter and chocolate in medium microwave-safe bowl. Microwave at MEDIUM (50%) 1 minute; stir. If necessary, microwave an additional 15 seconds at a time, stirring after each heating, until chocolate is melted when stirred. Cool 5 minutes.

3. Beat eggs and vanilla in large bowl until foamy. Gradually beat in granulated sugar. Blend in chocolate mixture; fold in flour and pecans. Spread mixture in prepared pan. Bake 40 to 45 minutes or until wooden pick inserted in center comes out clean. Cool completely in pan on wire rack.

4. Use foil to lift brownie from pan; remove foil. Place brownie layer on serving plate. Beat cream cheese and powdered sugar in medium bowl until well blended. Beat whipping cream and instant coffee until stiff; gradually fold into cream cheese mixture, blending well. Spread over brownie layer. Cover; refrigerate until serving time.

5. Just before serving, prepare CHOCOLATE GLAZE. Drizzle generous tablespoon glaze over top and down sides of each serving.

CHOCOLATE GLAZE

Place 6 ounces (1½ 4-ounce bars) HERSHEY'S SPECIAL DARK Chocolate Premium Baking Bar and ½ cup whipping cream in small microwave-safe bowl. Microwave at MEDIUM (50%) 30 to 45 seconds or until chocolate is melted and mixture is smooth when stirred. Cool slightly.

MAKES 1 CUP GLAZE ■

easy chocolate cream-filled torte

MAKES 8 TO 10 SERVINGS

1 frozen pound cake (10¾ ounces), thawed

½ cup powdered sugar

¼ cup HERSHEY'S Cocoa

1 cup (½ pint) cold whipping cream

1 teaspoon vanilla extract

CHOCOLATE GLAZE (recipe follows)

Sliced almonds (optional)

1. Cut cake horizontally to make 4 layers. Stir together sugar and cocoa in medium bowl. Add whipping cream and vanilla; beat until stiff.

2. Place bottom cake layer on serving platter. Spread ⅓ of the whipped cream mixture on cake layer. Place next cake layer on top of mixture; continue layering whipped cream mixture and cake until all have been used.

3. Prepare CHOCOLATE GLAZE; spoon over top of cake, allowing to drizzle down sides. Garnish with almonds, if desired. Refrigerate until ready to serve. Cover; refrigerate leftover torte.

CHOCOLATE GLAZE

2 tablespoons butter or margarine

2 tablespoons HERSHEY'S Cocoa

2 tablespoons water

1 cup powdered sugar

¼ to ½ teaspoon almond extract

1. Melt butter in small saucepan over low heat. Add cocoa and water. Cook, stirring constantly, until smooth and slightly thickened. Do not boil.

2. Remove from heat. Gradually add powdered sugar and almond extract, beating with whisk until smooth.

MAKES ABOUT ½ CUP GLAZE ■

toffee bread pudding
with cinnamon toffee sauce

MAKES 12 SERVINGS

1⅓ cups (8-ounce package) HEATH BITS 'O BRICKLE Toffee Bits, divided

3 cups milk

4 eggs

¾ cup sugar

¾ teaspoon ground cinnamon

¾ teaspoon vanilla extract

½ teaspoon salt

6 to 6½ cups ½-inch cubes French, Italian or sourdough bread

CINNAMON TOFFEE SAUCE (recipe follows)

Sweetened whipped cream or ice cream (optional)

1. Heat oven to 350°F. Butter 13×9×2-inch baking pan. Set aside ¾ cup toffee bits for sauce.

2. Mix together milk, eggs, sugar, cinnamon, vanilla and salt in large bowl with wire whisk. Stir in bread cubes, coating completely. Allow to stand 10 minutes. Stir in remaining toffee bits. Pour into prepared pan.

3. Bake 40 to 45 minutes or until surface is set. Cool 30 minutes.

4. Meanwhile, prepare CINNAMON TOFFEE SAUCE. Cut pudding into squares; top with sauce and sweetened whipped cream or ice cream, if desired.

CINNAMON TOFFEE SAUCE

Combine ¾ cup reserved toffee bits, ⅓ cup whipping cream and ⅛ teaspoon ground cinnamon in medium saucepan. Cook over low heat, stirring constantly, until toffee melts and mixture is well blended. (As toffee melts, small bits of almond will remain.)

MAKES ABOUT ⅔ CUP SAUCE

NOTE

This dessert is best eaten the same day it is prepared. ■

CREATIVE

CANDIES & SWEETS

SWEET EUPHORIA

filled chocolate meringues

2 egg whites, at room temperature

¼ teaspoon cream of tartar

Dash salt

½ cup sugar

½ teaspoon vanilla extract

2 tablespoons HERSHEY'S Cocoa

CHOCOLATE-CHEESE FILLING (recipe follows)

Raspberries and mint leaves for garnish

1. Heat oven to 275°F. Place parchment paper on cookie sheets.

2. Beat egg whites with cream of tartar and salt in medium bowl until soft peaks form. Beat in sugar, 1 tablespoon at a time, until stiff, glossy peaks form. Fold in vanilla. Sift cocoa over top of egg white mixture; gently fold in cocoa until combined. Drop by tablespoonfuls onto parchment paper. With back of small spoon, make indentation in center of each mound.

3. Bake 45 minutes or until meringue turns a light cream color and feels dry to the touch. Cool slightly; carefully peel meringues off parchment paper; cool completely on wire racks. To serve, spoon or pipe about 2 teaspoons CHOCOLATE-CHEESE FILLING into center of each meringue. Garnish each with a raspberry and a mint leaf.

Try growing your own mint—it adds a refreshing flavor to foods, while working great as a garnish.

CHOCOLATE-CHEESE FILLING

Combine 1 cup part-skim ricotta cheese, 2 tablespoons HERSHEY'S Cocoa, 1 tablespoon sugar and ½ teaspoon vanilla extract in food processor; blend until smooth. Cover; refrigerate.

MAKES 1 CUP FILLING ■

REESE'S peanut butter bark

MAKES ABOUT 1 POUND CANDY

2 packages (4 ounces each)
HERSHEY'S SPECIAL DARK Chocolate
Premium Baking Bars,
broken into pieces

1⅔ cups (10-ounce package)
REESE'S Peanut Butter Chips

1 tablespoon shortening
(do not use butter, margarine,
spread or oil)

½ cup roasted peanuts or toasted
almonds,* coarsely chopped

***To toast almonds: Heat oven to
350°F. Spread almonds in thin layer
in shallow baking pan. Bake 8 to
10 minutes, stirring occasionally,
until light golden brown; cool.**

1. Cover tray with wax paper.

2. Place chocolate in medium microwave-safe bowl. Microwave at MEDIUM (50%) 1 minute; stir. If necessary, microwave at MEDIUM an additional 30 seconds at a time, stirring after each heating, until chocolate is melted and smooth when stirred.

3. Immediately place peanut butter chips and shortening in second microwave-safe bowl. Microwave at MEDIUM (50%) 1 minute; stir. If necessary, microwave at MEDIUM an additional 30 seconds at a time, stirring after each heating, until chips are melted and mixture is smooth when stirred; stir in peanuts.

4. Alternately spoon above mixtures onto prepared tray; swirl with knife for marbled effect. Cover; refrigerate until firm. Break into pieces. ■

chocolate-covered banana pops

MAKES 9 POPS

3 ripe large bananas

9 wooden popsicle sticks

2 cups (12-ounce package) HERSHEY'S SPECIAL DARK Chocolate Chips or HERSHEY'S Semi-Sweet Chocolate Chips

2 tablespoons shortening (do not use butter, margarine, spread or oil)

1½ cups coarsely chopped unsalted, roasted peanuts

1. Peel bananas; cut each into thirds. Insert a wooden stick into each banana piece; place on wax paper-covered tray. Cover; freeze until firm.

2. Place chocolate chips and shortening in medium microwave-safe bowl. Microwave at MEDIUM (50%) 1½ to 2 minutes or until chocolate is melted and mixture is smooth when stirred.

3. Remove bananas from freezer just before dipping. Dip each piece into warm chocolate, covering completely; allow excess to drip off. Immediately roll in peanuts. Cover; return to freezer. Serve frozen.

VARIATION

HERSHEY'S Milk Chocolate Chips or HERSHEY'S Mini Chips Semi-Sweet Chocolate may be substituted for HERSHEY'S SPECIAL DARK Chocolate Chips or HERSHEY'S Semi-Sweet Chocolate Chips. ▪

chocolate and orange meltaways

2 cups (12-ounce package) HERSHEY'S Premier White Chips

½ cup (1 stick) unsalted butter (do not substitute margarine)

⅓ cup whipping cream

1½ teaspoons orange extract

CHOCOLATE COATING (recipe follows)

½ teaspoon shortening (do not use butter, margarine, spread or oil)

1. Line tray with wax paper. Reserve 2 tablespoons white chips.

2. Combine butter and whipping cream in medium saucepan; cook over low heat, stirring constantly until mixture comes to a full rolling boil. Remove from heat; immediately add remaining white chips. Stir with whisk until smooth. Add orange extract; blend well.

3. Refrigerate until firm enough to handle, about 2 hours. Taking small amount of mixture at a time, shape into 1-inch balls. Place on prepared tray; refrigerate until firm, about 1½ hours. Prepare CHOCOLATE COATING. Place 1 candy onto fork; dip into coating, covering completely and allowing excess to drip off. Place candies onto prepared tray. Repeat with remaining candies. Refrigerate until coating is set, about 1 hour.

4. Place reserved 2 tablespoons white chips and shortening in small microwave-safe bowl. Microwave at MEDIUM (50%) 30 seconds; stir. If necessary, microwave at MEDIUM an additional 10 seconds or until mixture is smooth when stirred. With fork, lightly drizzle over coated candies; refrigerate until set, about 20 minutes. Cover; store in refrigerator.

CHOCOLATE COATING

Place 2 packages (4 ounces each) HERSHEY'S SPECIAL DARK Chocolate Premium Baking Bar, broken into pieces and 1 teaspoon shortening (do not use butter, margarine, spread or oil) in medium microwave-safe bowl. Microwave at MEDIUM (50%) 2 minutes; stir. If necessary, microwave at MEDIUM an additional 15 seconds at a time, stirring after each heating, until chocolate is melted and mixture is smooth when stirred. Cool slightly. (If chocolate is too hot, it will not coat candy. ■

butterscotch nut fudge

MAKES ABOUT 5 DOZEN PIECES OR ABOUT 2¼ POUNDS CANDY

- 1¾ cups sugar
- 1 jar (7 ounces) marshmallow crème
- ¾ cup evaporated milk
- ¼ cup (½ stick) butter
- 1¾ cups (11-ounce package) HERSHEY'S Butterscotch Chips
- 1 cup chopped salted mixed nuts
- 1 teaspoon vanilla extract

1. Line 8-inch square pan with foil, extending foil over edges of pan.

2. Combine sugar, marshmallow crème, evaporated milk and butter in heavy 3-quart saucepan. Cook over medium heat, stirring constantly, until mixture comes to a full boil; boil and stir 5 minutes.

3. Remove from heat; gradually add butterscotch chips, stirring until chips are melted. Stir in nuts and vanilla. Pour into prepared pan; cool.

4. Refrigerate 2 to 3 hours. Remove from pan; place on cutting board. Peel off foil. Cut into squares. Store tightly covered in refrigerator.

NOTE

For best results, do not double recipe. ■

white & chocolate covered strawberries

2 cups (12-ounce package) HERSHEY'S Premier White Chips

2 tablespoons shortening (do not use butter, margarine, spread or oil), divided

4 cups (2 pints) fresh strawberries, rinsed, patted dry and chilled

1 cup HERSHEY'S SPECIAL DARK Chocolate Chips or HERSHEY'S Semi-Sweet Chocolate Chips

1. Cover tray with wax paper.

2. Place white chips and 1 tablespoon shortening in medium microwave-safe bowl. Microwave at MEDIUM (50%) 1 minute; stir until chips are melted and mixture is smooth. If necessary, microwave at MEDIUM an additional 15 seconds at a time, just until smooth when stirred.

3. Holding by top, dip ⅓ of each strawberry into white chip mixture; shake gently to remove excess. Place on prepared tray; refrigerate until coating is firm, at least 30 minutes.

4. Repeat microwave procedure with chocolate chips and remaining shortening in clean microwave-safe bowl. Dip lower ⅓ of each berry into chocolate mixture. Refrigerate until firm. Cover; refrigerate leftover strawberries. ■

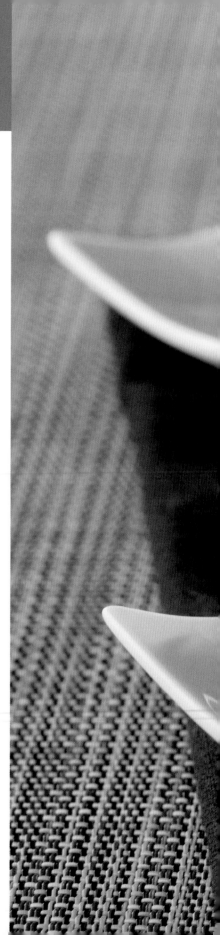

chocolate peanut clusters

MAKES ABOUT 2 DOZEN CANDIES

½ cup HERSHEY'S Milk Chocolate Chips

½ cup HERSHEY'S SPECIAL DARK Chocolate Chips or HERSHEY'S Semi-Sweet Chocolate Chips

1 tablespoon shortening (do not use butter, margarine, spread or oil)

1 cup unsalted, roasted peanuts

1. Place milk chocolate chips, SPECIAL DARK chocolate chips and shortening in small microwave-safe bowl. Microwave at MEDIUM (50%) 1 to 1½ minutes or just until chips are melted and mixture is smooth when stirred. Stir in peanuts.

2. Drop by teaspoons into 1-inch diameter candy or petit four papers. Refrigerate until firm, about 1 hour. Store in airtight container in cool, dry place. ■

chocolate buttercream cherry candies

MAKES ABOUT 48 CANDIES

About 48 maraschino cherries with stems, well drained

¼ cup (½ stick) butter, softened

2 cups powdered sugar

¼ cup HERSHEY'S Cocoa or HERSHEY'S SPECIAL DARK Cocoa

1 to 2 tablespoons milk, divided

½ teaspoon vanilla extract

¼ teaspoon almond extract

WHITE CHIP COATING (recipe follows)

CHOCOLATE CHIP DRIZZLE (recipe follows)

1. Cover tray with wax paper. Lightly press cherries between layers of paper towels to remove excess moisture.

2. Beat butter, powdered sugar, cocoa and 1 tablespoon milk in small bowl until well blended; stir in vanilla and almond extract. If necessary, add remaining milk, 1 teaspoon at a time, until mixture will hold together but is not wet.

3. Mold scant teaspoon mixture around each cherry, covering completely; place on prepared tray. Cover; refrigerate 3 hours or until firm.

4. Prepare WHITE CHIP COATING. Holding each cherry by stem, dip into coating. Place on tray; refrigerate until firm.

5. About 1 hour before serving, prepare CHOCOLATE CHIP DRIZZLE; with tines of fork drizzle randomly over candies. Refrigerate until drizzle is firm. Store in refrigerator.

WHITE CHIP COATING

Place 2 cups (12-ounce package) HERSHEY'S Premier White Chips in small microwave-safe bowl; drizzle with 2 tablespoons vegetable oil. Microwave at MEDIUM (50%) 1 minute; stir. If necessary, microwave at MEDIUM an additional 15 seconds at a time, stirring after each heating just until chips are melted and mixture is smooth. If mixture thickens while coating, microwave at MEDIUM 15 seconds; stir until smooth.

A chocolate drizzle makes a quick and classy finish to candies, cookies, cakes, and other desserts.

CHOCOLATE CHIP DRIZZLE

Place ¼ cup HERSHEY'S SPECIAL DARK Chocolate Chips or HERSHEY'S Semi-Sweet Chocolate Chips and ¼ teaspoon shortening (do not use butter, margarine, spread or oil) in another small microwave-safe bowl. Microwave at MEDIUM (50%) 30 seconds to 1 minute; stir until chips are melted and mixture is smooth. ■

KISSES fluted cups with peanut butter filling

MAKES ABOUT 2 DOZEN PIECES

72 HERSHEY'S KISSES BRAND Milk Chocolates, divided

1 cup REESE'S Creamy Peanut Butter

1 cup powdered sugar

1 tablespoon butter or margarine, softened

1. Line 24 small muffin cups (1¾ inches in diameter) with small paper bake cups. Remove wrappers from chocolates.

2. Place 48 chocolates in small microwave-safe bowl. Microwave at MEDIUM (50%) 1 minute; stir. Microwave at MEDIUM an additional 10 seconds at a time, stirring after each heating, just until chocolate is melted when stirred. Using small brush, coat inside of paper cups with melted chocolate.

3. Refrigerate 20 minutes; reapply melted chocolate to any thin spots. Refrigerate until firm, preferably overnight. Gently peel paper from chocolate cups.

4. Beat peanut butter, powdered sugar and butter with electric mixer on medium speed in small bowl until smooth. Spoon into chocolate cups. Before serving, top each cup with a chocolate piece. Cover; store cups in refrigerator. ■

christmas KISSES candies

MAKES ABOUT 14 CANDIES

About 14 HERSHEY'S KISSES BRAND Milk Chocolates

¾ cup ground almonds

⅓ cup powdered sugar

1 tablespoon light corn syrup

½ teaspoon almond extract

Few drops green food color

Few drops red food color

Granulated sugar

1. Remove wrappers from chocolates. Stir together ground almonds and powdered sugar in medium bowl until well blended. Stir together corn syrup and almond extract; pour over almond mixture, stirring until completely blended. Divide mixture in half, placing each half in separate bowls.

2. Add green food color to one part; with hands, mix until color is well blended and mixture clings together. Add red food color to other half; mix as directed.

3. Shape at least 1 teaspoon colored almond mixture around each chocolate. Roll in granulated sugar. ■

SPECIAL
OCCASIONS &
CELEBRATIONS

FOR THE LOVE
OF CHOCOLATE

chocolate mousse cake roll

MAKES 8 TO 10 SERVINGS

CHOCOLATE MOUSSE FILLING
(recipe follows)

4 eggs, separated

½ cup plus ⅓ cup granulated sugar, divided

1 teaspoon vanilla extract

½ cup all-purpose flour

⅓ cup HERSHEY'S Cocoa

½ teaspoon baking powder

¼ teaspoon baking soda

⅛ teaspoon salt

⅓ cup water

Powdered sugar

HERSHEY'S Syrup

1. Prepare CHOCOLATE MOUSSE FILLING. Chill 6 to 8 hours or overnight.

2. Prepare cake.* Heat oven to 375°F. Line 15½×10½×1-inch jelly-roll pan with foil; generously grease foil.

3. Beat egg whites in large bowl until soft peaks form; gradually add ½ cup granulated sugar, beating until stiff peaks form. Beat egg yolks and vanilla in medium bowl on medium speed of mixer 3 minutes. Gradually add remaining ⅓ cup granulated sugar; continue beating 2 additional minutes.

4. Stir together flour, cocoa, baking powder, baking soda and salt; add to egg yolk mixture alternately with water, beating on low speed just until batter is smooth. Gradually fold chocolate mixture into beaten egg whites until well blended. Spread batter evenly in prepared pan.

5. Bake 12 to 15 minutes or until top springs back when touched lightly in center. Immediately loosen cake from edges of pan; invert onto clean towel sprinkled with powdered sugar. Carefully peel off foil. Immediately roll cake and towel together starting from narrow end; place on wire rack to cool completely.

6. Carefully unroll cake; remove towel. Gently stir filling until of spreading consistency. Spread cake with filling; reroll cake. Refrigerate several hours. Sift powdered sugar over top just before serving. Serve drizzled with syrup and garnish as desired. Cover; refrigerate leftover cake roll.

*Cake may be prepared up to two days in advance. Keep cake rolled tightly and covered well so that it doesn't get dry.

CHOCOLATE MOUSSE FILLING

¼ cup sugar

1 teaspoon unflavored gelatin

½ cup milk

1 cup HERSHEY'S SPECIAL DARK Chocolate Chips or HERSHEY'S Semi-Sweet Chocolate Chips

2 teaspoons vanilla extract

1 cup (½ pint) cold whipping cream

1. Stir together sugar and gelatin in small saucepan; stir in milk. Let stand 2 minutes to soften gelatin. Cook over medium heat, stirring constantly, until mixture just begins to boil.

2. Remove from heat. Immediately add chocolate chips; stir until melted. Stir in vanilla; cool to room temperature.

3. Beat whipping cream in small bowl until stiff. Gradually add chocolate mixture, folding gently just until blended. Cover; refrigerate until ready to use. ■

SPECIAL DARK
chocolate chip scones

MAKES 24 SCONES

3¼ cups all-purpose flour

½ cup granulated sugar

1 tablespoon plus 1 teaspoon baking powder

¼ teaspoon salt

2 cups (12-ounce package) HERSHEY'S SPECIAL DARK Chocolate Chips

½ cup chopped nuts (optional)

2 cups whipping cream, chilled

2 tablespoons butter, melted

Additional granulated sugar

Powdered sugar (optional)

1. Heat oven to 375°F. Lightly grease 2 baking sheets.

2. Stir together flour, ½ cup granulated sugar, baking powder and salt in large bowl. Stir in chocolate chips and nuts, if desired.

3. Stir whipping cream into flour mixture just until ingredients are moistened.

4. Turn mixture out onto lightly floured surface. Knead gently until soft dough forms, about 2 minutes. Divide dough into three equal balls. One ball at a time, flatten into 7-inch circle; cut into 8 triangles. Transfer triangles to prepared baking sheets, spacing 2 inches apart. Brush with melted butter and sprinkle with additional granulated sugar.

5. Bake 15 to 20 minutes or until lightly browned. Serve warm, sprinkled with powdered sugar, if desired. ▪

HERSHEY'S KISSES birthday cake

MAKES 10 TO 12 SERVINGS

2 cups sugar

1¾ cups all-purpose flour

¾ cup HERSHEY'S Cocoa or
HERSHEY'S SPECIAL DARK Cocoa

1½ teaspoons baking powder

1½ teaspoons baking soda

1 teaspoon salt

2 eggs

1 cup milk

½ cup vegetable oil

2 teaspoons vanilla extract

1 cup boiling water

VANILLA BUTTERCREAM FROSTING
(recipe follows)

HERSHEY'S KISSES BRAND
Milk Chocolates

1. Heat oven to 350°F. Grease and flour two 9-inch round baking pans or one 13×9×2-inch baking pan.

2. Stir together sugar, flour, cocoa, baking powder, baking soda and salt in large bowl. Add eggs, milk, oil and vanilla; beat with electric mixer on medium speed for 2 minutes. Stir in boiling water (batter will be thin). Pour batter into prepared pans.

3. Bake 30 to 35 minutes for round pans, 35 to 40 minutes for rectangular pan or until wooden pick inserted in center comes out clean. Cool 10 minutes; turn out onto wire racks. Cool completely.

4. Frost with VANILLA BUTTERCREAM FROSTING. Remove wrappers from chocolates. Garnish top and sides of cake with chocolates.

VANILLA BUTTERCREAM FROSTING

⅓ cup butter or margarine, softened

4 cups powdered sugar, divided

3 to 4 tablespoons milk

1½ teaspoons vanilla extract

Beat butter with electric mixer on medium speed in large bowl until creamy. With mixer running, gradually add about 2 cups powdered sugar, beating until well blended. Slowly beat in milk and vanilla. Gradually add remaining powdered sugar, beating until smooth. Add additional milk, if necessary, until frosting is desired consistency.

MAKES ABOUT 2⅓ CUPS FROSTING ■

easy easter KISSES & peanut butter cup pie

16 REESE'S Peanut Butter Cups Miniatures, unwrapped and chopped

5¼ cups (12 ounces) frozen nondairy whipped topping, thawed and divided

2 tablespoons REESE'S Creamy Peanut Butter

1 prepared (6 ounce) graham cracker crumb crust

27 HERSHEY'S KISSES BRAND Milk Chocolates, unwrapped

24 REESE'S Peanut Butter Cups Miniatures or HERSHEY'S KISSES BRAND Milk Chocolates, unwrapped

24 HERSHEY'S Candy-Coated Milk Chocolate Eggs

1. Combine chopped peanut butter cups, 2 cups whipped topping and creamy peanut butter in large bowl. Spread onto bottom of crumb crust.

2. Place 27 HERSHEY'S KISSES BRAND Milk Chocolates in small microwave-safe bowl. Microwave at MEDIUM (50%) 1 minute; stir. If necessary, microwave at MEDIUM an additional 15 seconds at a time, stirring after each heating, until chocolate is melted and smooth when stirred. Stir in 2 cups whipped topping; spread on top of peanut butter layer. Cover; refrigerate until firm.

3. Spread remaining 1¼ cups whipped topping on top of pie. Cut into slices and decorate each slice with 3 chocolates and 3 candy eggs. Serve immediately; refrigerate leftovers. ■

holiday chocolate cake

MAKES 10 TO 12 SERVINGS

2 cups sugar

1¾ cups all-purpose flour

¾ cup HERSHEY'S Cocoa

2 teaspoons baking soda

1 teaspoon baking powder

1 teaspoon salt

1 cup buttermilk or sour milk*

1 cup strong black coffee or 2 teaspoons instant coffee dissolved in 1 cup hot water

½ cup vegetable oil

2 eggs

2 teaspoons vanilla extract

RICOTTA CHEESE FILLING (recipe follows)

CHOCOLATE WHIPPED CREAM (recipe follows)

VANILLA WHIPPED CREAM (recipe follows)

Candied red or green cherries (optional)

*To sour milk: Use 1 tablespoon white vinegar plus milk to equal 1 cup.

1. Heat oven to 350°F. Grease and flour two 9-inch round baking pans.

2. Stir together sugar, flour, cocoa, baking soda, baking powder and salt in large bowl. Add buttermilk, coffee, oil, eggs and vanilla; beat at medium speed of mixer 2 minutes (batter will be thin). Pour batter into prepared pans.

3. Bake 30 to 35 minutes or until wooden pick inserted into centers of cakes comes out clean. Cool 10 minutes; remove from pans to wire racks. Cool completely.

4. Slice cake layers in half horizontally. Place bottom slice on serving plate; top with ⅓ RICOTTA CHEESE FILLING. Alternate cake layers and filling, ending with cake on top. Frost cake with CHOCOLATE WHIPPED CREAM. Decorate with VANILLA WHIPPED CREAM and cherries, if desired. Cover; refrigerate leftover cake.

RICOTTA CHEESE FILLING

1¾ cups (15 ounces) ricotta cheese*

¼ cup sugar

3 tablespoons Grand Marnier (orange-flavored liqueur) or orange juice concentrate, undiluted

¼ cup candied red or green cherries, coarsely chopped

⅓ cup HERSHEY'S Mini Chips Semi-Sweet Chocolate

Beat ricotta cheese, sugar and liqueur in large bowl until smooth. Fold in candied cherries and small chocolate chips.

*1 cup (½ pint) whipping cream can be substituted for ricotta cheese. Beat with sugar and liqueur until stiff. Fold in candied cherries and small chocolate chips.

CHOCOLATE WHIPPED CREAM

Stir together ⅓ cup powdered sugar and 2 tablespoons HERSHEY'S Cocoa in small bowl. Add 1 cup (½ pint) cold whipping cream and 1 teaspoon vanilla extract; beat until stiff.

VANILLA WHIPPED CREAM

Beat ½ cup cold whipping cream, 2 tablespoons powdered sugar and ½ teaspoon vanilla extract in small bowl until stiff. ■

MINI KISSES
pumpkin mousse cups

MAKES 10 SERVINGS

1¾ cups (10-ounce package) HERSHEY'S MINI KISSES BRAND Milk Chocolates, divided

24 marshmallows

½ cup milk

½ cup canned pumpkin

1 teaspoon vanilla extract

1 teaspoon pumpkin pie spice

⅓ cup powdered sugar

1 cup (½ pint) cold whipping cream

1. Line 10 muffin cups (2½ inches in diameter) with paper bake cups. Reserve ½ cup chocolate pieces. Place remaining 1¼ cups chocolates in small microwave-safe bowl; microwave at MEDIUM (50%) 1 minute or until melted when stirred. Mixture should be thick.

2. Very thickly coat inside pleated surfaces and bottoms of bake cups with melted chocolate using soft pastry brush. Refrigerate 10 minutes; recoat any thin spots with melted chocolate.* Refrigerate until firm, about 2 hours. Gently peel off paper; refrigerate until ready to fill.

3. Place marshmallows, milk and pumpkin in medium microwave-safe bowl. Microwave at MEDIUM (50%) 1 minute; stir. Microwave additional 30 seconds at a time, stirring after each heating, until mixture is melted and smooth. Stir in vanilla and pumpkin pie spice. Cool completely.

4. Beat powdered sugar and whipping cream until stiff; fold into pumpkin mixture. Fill cups with pumpkin mousse; garnish with whipped cream and reserved chocolates pieces. Cover; refrigerate 2 hours or until firm.

*If reheating is needed, microwave chocolate at MEDIUM (50%) 15 seconds; stir. ∎

holiday coconut cake

COCONUT CAKE

½ cup (1 stick) butter or margarine, softened

½ cup shortening

2 cups granulated sugar

5 eggs, separated

1 teaspoon vanilla extract

2 cups all-purpose flour

1 teaspoon baking soda

¼ teaspoon salt

1 cup buttermilk

2 cups MOUNDS Sweetened Coconut Flakes

½ cup chopped pecans

TOFFEE CREAM

2 cups cold whipping cream

¼ cup powdered sugar

1 teaspoon vanilla extract

½ cup HEATH BITS 'O BRICKLE Toffee Bits

Additional HEATH BITS 'O BRICKLE Toffee Bits (optional)

1. Heat oven to 350°F. Grease and flour 12-cup fluted tube pan.

2. Beat butter, shortening, granulated sugar, egg yolks and vanilla with electric mixer on medium speed in large bowl until creamy. Stir together flour, baking soda and salt; add alternately with buttermilk, beating until well blended. Stir in coconut and pecans.

3. Beat egg whites with electric mixer on high speed in large bowl until stiff peaks form; fold into batter. Pour batter into prepared pan.

4. Bake 45 to 55 minutes or until wooden pick inserted in center comes out clean. Cool 10 minutes; remove from pan to wire rack. Cool completely.

5. For TOFFEE CREAM, beat whipping cream, powdered sugar and vanilla extract with electric mixer on medium speed in large bowl until stiff peaks form. Fold in toffee bits. Frost cake with TOFFEE CREAM. Garnish with additional toffee bits, if desired. Cover; store leftover cake in refrigerator. ■

holiday fudge torte

1 cup all-purpose flour

¾ cup sugar

¼ cup HERSHEY'S Cocoa

1½ teaspoons powdered instant coffee

¾ teaspoon baking soda

¼ teaspoon salt

½ cup (1 stick) butter or margarine, softened

¾ cup dairy sour cream

1 egg

½ teaspoon vanilla extract

FUDGE NUT GLAZE (recipe follows)

1. Heat oven to 350°F. Grease 9-inch round baking pan; line bottom with wax paper. Grease paper; flour paper and pan.

2. Stir together flour, sugar, cocoa, instant coffee, baking soda and salt in large bowl. Add butter, sour cream, egg and vanilla; beat on low speed of mixer until blended. Increase speed to medium; beat 3 minutes. Pour batter into prepared pan.

3. Bake 30 to 35 minutes or until wooden pick inserted in center comes out clean. Cool 10 minutes. Remove from pan to wire rack; gently peel off wax paper. Cool completely.

4. Prepare FUDGE NUT GLAZE.

5. Place cake on serving plate; pour glaze evenly over cake, allowing some to run down sides. Refrigerate until glaze is firm, about 1 hour. Cover; refrigerate leftover torte.

FUDGE NUT GLAZE

½ cup whipping cream

¼ cup sugar

1 tablespoon butter

1½ teaspoons light corn syrup

⅓ cup HERSHEY'S SPECIAL DARK Chocolate Chips or HERSHEY'S Semi-Sweet Chocolate Chips

¾ cup chopped MAUNA LOA Macadamia Nuts, hazelnuts or pecans

½ teaspoon vanilla extract

1. Combine all ingredients except nuts and vanilla in small saucepan. Cook over medium heat, stirring constantly, until mixture boils. Cook, stirring constantly, 5 minutes. Remove from heat.

2. Cool 10 minutes; stir in nuts and vanilla. ■

drinking chocolate

2 sections (½ ounce each)
HERSHEY'S Unsweetened Chocolate
Premium Baking Bar

2 tablespoons hot water

¼ cup sugar

Dash of salt

¼ cup milk, warmed

¼ teaspoon vanilla extract

Place chocolate and water in top of small double boiler. Melt over simmering water, stirring until smooth. Stir in sugar and salt, blending thoroughly. Gradually blend in warm milk. Heat, stirring occasionally, until hot. Stir in vanilla. Pour into demitasse cups. Garnish as desired. Serve immediately. ■

holiday double peanut butter fudge cookies

MAKES ABOUT 3½ DOZEN COOKIES

1 can (14 ounces) sweetened condensed milk (not evaporated milk)

¾ cup REESE'S Creamy Peanut Butter

2 cups all-purpose biscuit baking mix

1 teaspoon vanilla extract

¾ cup REESE'S Peanut Butter Chips

¼ cup granulated sugar

½ teaspoon red colored sugar

½ teaspoon green colored sugar

1. Heat oven to 375°F.

2. Beat sweetened condensed milk and peanut butter in large bowl with electric mixer on medium speed until smooth. Beat in baking mix and vanilla; stir in peanut butter chips. Set aside.

3. Stir together granulated sugar and colored sugars in small bowl. Shape dough into 1-inch balls; roll in sugar. Place 2 inches apart on ungreased cookie sheet; flatten slightly with bottom of glass.

4. Bake 6 to 8 minutes or until very lightly browned (do not overbake). Cool slightly. Remove to wire rack and cool completely. Store in tightly covered container. ■

MAKES 24 SERVINGS

2 packages (18¼ ounces each) white cake mix, divided

2½ cups water, divided

⅔ cup vegetable oil, divided

4 eggs

½ cup sugar, divided

¼ cup HERSHEY'S Cocoa, divided

PREMIER WHITE BUTTERCREAM FROSTING (recipe follows)

CHOCOLATE BUTTERCREAM FROSTING (recipe follows)

2 packages (10 ounces each) HERSHEY'S MINI KISSES BRAND Milk Chocolates

MILK CHOCOLATE FILIGREE HEARTS (recipe follows)

1. Heat oven to 350°F. Grease and flour 8-inch square baking pan and 8-inch round baking pan. Line bottoms with wax paper; grease and flour paper.

2. Place contents of 1 package cake mix, 1¼ cups water, ⅓ cup vegetable oil and 2 eggs in large bowl; beat until blended. Place 1 cup batter in small bowl; stir in ¼ cup sugar and 2 tablespoons cocoa until blended. Divide vanilla batter evenly into prepared pans; spoon cocoa batter in dollops over top of batter in pans. With knife or spatula, marble chocolate through vanilla batter.

3. Bake 30 to 35 minutes or until wooden pick inserted in center comes out clean. Cool 15 minutes; remove cakes from pans. Remove wax paper; cool completely.

4. Repeat steps 1, 2 and 3.

5. Prepare PREMIER WHITE BUTTERCREAM FROSTING and CHOCOLATE BUTTERCREAM FROSTING. To assemble cake, cover 18×14-inch heavy cardboard with foil. Cut both round layers in half vertically. Arrange 1 square and 2 semi-circles into heart shape. Spread with small amount of frosting; place other square and 2 semi-circles on top. Frost top with white frosting; frost sides with chocolate frosting. Outline entire top and bottom edges of heart-shaped cake with chocolate pieces. Garnish with MILK CHOCOLATE FILIGREE HEARTS, if desired.

PREMIER WHITE BUTTERCREAM FROSTING

2 cups (12-ounce package) HERSHEY'S Premier White Chips

⅓ cup milk

1½ cups (3 sticks) cold butter, cut into pieces

1¾ cups powdered sugar

1. Place white chips and milk in large microwave-safe bowl. Microwave at MEDIUM (50%) 1 minute; stir. If necessary, microwave an additional 30 seconds at a time, until mixture is melted and smooth when stirred; cool to lukewarm.

2. Beat butter and powdered sugar gradually into white chip mixture; beat until fluffy.

MAKES ABOUT 4 CUPS FROSTING

CHOCOLATE BUTTERCREAM FROSTING

In bowl, place 2 cups PREMIER WHITE BUTTERCREAM FROSTING; beat in 2 tablespoons HERSHEY'S Cocoa.

MILK CHOCOLATE FILIGREE HEARTS

1 cup HERSHEY'S MINI KISSES BRAND Milk Chocolates

1. Draw desired size heart shapes on paper; cover with wax paper. Place both sheets of paper on baking sheet or tray.

2. Place chocolate pieces in microwave-safe bowl. Microwave at MEDIUM (50%) 30 seconds or just until chocolate is melted when stirred.

3. Pour melted chocolate in small, heavy seal-top plastic bag. With scissors, make small diagonal cut in bottom corner of bag. Pipe thick outlines of heart shapes following heart outlines; fill in center of hearts with a crisscross of chocolate to connect the sides. Refrigerate until firm.

4. Carefully peel wax paper away from chocolate hearts. Place on tray; cover and refrigerate until ready to use as garnishes for cake. ■

holiday red raspberry chocolate bars

MAKES 36 BARS

2½ cups all-purpose flour

1 cup sugar

¾ cup finely chopped pecans

1 egg, beaten

1 cup (2 sticks) cold butter or margarine

1 jar (12 ounces) seedless red raspberry jam

1⅔ cups HERSHEY'S Milk Chocolate Chips, HERSHEY'S SPECIAL DARK Chocolate Chips, HERSHEY'S Semi-Sweet Chocolate Chips or HERSHEY'S MINI KISSES BRAND Milk Chocolates

1. Heat oven to 350°F. Grease 13×9×2-inch baking pan.

2. Stir together flour, sugar, pecans and egg in large bowl. Cut in butter with pastry blender or fork until mixture resembles coarse crumbs; set aside 1½ cups crumb mixture. Press remaining crumb mixture on bottom of prepared pan. Stir jam to soften; carefully spread over crumb mixture in pan. Sprinkle with chocolate chips. Crumble reserved crumb mixture evenly over top.

3. Bake 40 to 45 minutes or until lightly browned. Cool completely in pan on wire rack; cut into bars. ■

HERSHEY'S
chocolate peppermint roll

MAKES 10 TO 12 SERVINGS

CHOCOLATE SPONGE ROLL

4 eggs, separated

½ cup plus ⅓ cup granulated sugar, divided

1 teaspoon vanilla extract

½ cup all-purpose flour

⅓ cup HERSHEY'S Cocoa

½ teaspoon baking powder

¼ teaspoon baking soda

⅛ teaspoon salt

⅓ cup water

PEPPERMINT FILLING

1 cup whipping cream, cold

¼ cup powdered sugar

¼ cup finely crushed hard peppermint candy or ½ teaspoon mint extract

Few drops red food color (optional)

CHOCOLATE GLAZE

2 tablespoons butter or margarine

2 tablespoons HERSHEY'S Cocoa

2 tablespoons water

1 cup powdered sugar

⅓ teaspoon vanilla extract

1. For CHOCOLATE SPONGE ROLL, heat oven to 375°F. Line 15½×10½×1-inch jelly-roll pan with foil; generously grease foil.

2. Beat egg whites with electric mixer on high speed in large bowl until soft peaks form; gradually add ½ cup granulated sugar, beating until stiff peaks form. Set aside.

3. Beat egg yolks and vanilla with electric mixer on medium speed in medium bowl 3 minutes. Gradually add remaining ⅓ cup granulated sugar; continue beating 2 minutes. Stir together flour, cocoa, baking powder, baking soda and salt. With mixer on low speed, add flour mixture to egg yolk mixture alternately with water, beating just until batter is smooth. Using rubber spatula, gradually fold beaten egg whites into chocolate mixture until well blended. Spread batter evenly in prepared pan.

4. Bake 12 to 15 minutes or until top springs back when touched lightly. Immediately loosen cake from edges of pan; invert onto clean towel sprinkled with powdered sugar. Carefully peel off foil.

Drizzle a chocolate glaze over cakes and other desserts for the quick and perfect finishing touch.

Immediately roll cake in towel, starting from narrow end; place on wire rack to cool completely.

5. For PEPPERMINT FILLING, beat whipping cream with electric mixer on medium speed in medium bowl until slightly thickened. Add ¼ cup powdered sugar and peppermint candy or mint extract and food color, if desired; beat cream until stiff peaks form.

6. For CHOCOLATE GLAZE, melt butter in small saucepan over very low heat; add cocoa and water, stirring until smooth and slightly thickened. Remove from heat and cool slightly. (Cool completely for thicker frosting.) Gradually beat in 1 cup powdered sugar and vanilla extract.

7. Carefully unroll cake; remove towel. Spread cake with PEPPERMINT FILLING; reroll cake. Glaze with CHOCOLATE GLAZE. Refrigerate until just before serving. Cover; refrigerate leftover dessert. ■

INDEX

index

A

All-Chocolate Boston Cream Pie 124

Almond Shortbread Cookies with Chocolate Filling 38

Autumn Peanutty Carrot Cake 86

B

BARS & BROWNIES

Best Fudgey Pecan Brownies 60

Chewy Toffee Almond Bars 54

Chocolate Almond Macaroon Bars 46

Chocolate Fudge Pecan Pie Bars 44

Chocolate Orange Cheesecake Bars 58

Chocolate Seven Layer Bars 62

Chocolate Streusel Bars 68

Chunky Macadamia Bars 64

Cranberry Orange Ricotta Cheese Brownies 66

English Toffee Bars 70

Five Layer Bars 56

Holiday Red Raspberry Chocolate Bars 246

Mini Brownie Cups 18

MINI KISSES® BRAND Fruit Bars 52

Peanut Butter Fudge Brownie Bars 50

Peanut Butter Glazed Chocolate Bars 48

Best Fudgey Pecan Brownies 60

BEVERAGES

Drinking Chocolate 240

BREAKFASTS

HUGS & KISSES® BRAND Crescents 188

SPECIAL DARK® Chocolate Chip Scones 226

Butterscotch Nut Fudge 210

C

CAKES

Autumn Peanutty Carrot Cake 86

Chocolate Cake Fingers 80

Chocolate Cherry Delight Cake 76

Chocolate Lemon Marble Cake 92

Chocolate Mousse Cake Roll 224

Chocolate Syrup Swirl Cake 88

Collector's Cocoa Cake 74

European Mocha Fudge Cake 82

HERSHEY®S Chocolate Peppermint Roll 248

HERSHEY®S KISSES® BRAND Birthday Cake 228

HERSHEY®S Lavish Chocolate Cake 84

HERSHEY®S "PERFECTLY CHOCOLATE"
Chocolate Cake 100

HERSHEY®S SPECIAL DARK® Snack Cake Medley 98

Holiday Chocolate Cake 232

Holiday Coconut Cake 236

Mocha Molten Chocolate Cake 78

Shower Them with KISSES® BRAND Cake 244

Strawberry Chocolate Chip Shortcake 96

index

CANDIES

Butterscotch Nut Fudge 210

Chocolate-Covered Banana Pops 206

Chocolate and Orange Meltaways 208

Chocolate Buttercream Cherry Candies 216

Chocolate Peanut Clusters 214

Christmas KISSES® BRAND Candies 220

Filled Chocolate Meringues 202

KISSES® BRAND Fluted Cups with Peanut Butter Filling 218

REESE'S® Peanut Butter Bark 204

White & Chocolate Covered Strawberries 212

Cappuccino-KISSed Cheesecake 106

CHEESECAKES

Cappuccino-KISSed Cheesecake 106

Chilled Raspberry Cheesecake 104

Creamy Ambrosia Cheesecake 116

HERSHEY®S SPECIAL DARK® Chocolate Layered
Cheesecake 110

HERSHEY®S SPECIAL DARK® Truffle Brownie
Cheesecake 114

Peanut Butter Holiday Cheesecake 108

Triple Layer Cheesecake 112

Ultra Chocolate Cheesecake 118

Cherry-Glazed Chocolate Torte 164

Chewy Toffee Almond Bars 54

Chilled Raspberry Cheesecake 104

Chocolate-Covered Banana Pops 206

Chocolate Almond Macaroon Bars 46

Chocolate Almond Torte 94

Chocolate and Orange Meltaways 208

Chocolate and Vanilla-Swirled Cheese Pie 128

Chocolate Buttercream Cherry Candies 216

Chocolate Cake Fingers 80

Chocolate Cherry Delight Cake 76

Chocolate Chip & Toffee Bits Cookies 16

Chocolate Chip Cookie Dough Cheesepie 134

Chocolate Cups with Lemon Cream 162

Chocolate Dream Cups 186

Chocolate Fudge Pecan Pie Bars 44

Chocolate Lemon Marble Cake 92

Chocolate Magic Mousse Pie 140

Chocolate Marbled Peanut Butter Pie 138

Chocolate Mini-Puffs 160

Chocolate Mousse Cake Roll 224

Chocolate Orange Cheesecake Bars 58

Chocolate Peanut Clusters 214

Chocolate Raspberry Dessert 182

Chocolate Seven Layer Bars 62

Chocolate Streusel Bars 68

Chocolate Swirl Lollipop Cookies 26

Chocolate Syrup Swirl Cake 88

Chocolate Syrup Swirl Dessert 168

Christmas KISSES® BRAND Candies 220

Chunky Macadamia Bars 64

Classic Boston Cream Pie 144

Classic Chocolate Cream Pie 130

Collector's Cocoa Cake 74

COOKIES

Almond Shortbread Cookies with Chocolate Filling........ 38

Chocolate Chip & Toffee Bits Cookies 16

Chocolate Swirl Lollipop Cookies 26

Double Chocolate Coconut Oatmeal Cookies.................. 28

Double-Drizzled Chocolate Shortbread Cookies 20

HERSHEY®S Double Chocolate MINI KISSES® BRAND
Cookies.. 40

Holiday Double Peanut Butter Fudge Cookies.............. 242

KISSES® BRAND Macaroon Cookies... 30

MINI KISSES® BRAND Milk Chocolate Peanut Butter
Cookies.. 22

Peanut Butter Blossoms 34

Peanut Butter Cut-Out Cookies 32

Pecan MINI KISSES® BRAND Cups 24

Rich Cocoa Crinkle Cookies 36

Secret KISSES® BRAND Cookies.. 14

Cranberry Orange Ricotta Cheese Brownies 66

Creamy Ambrosia Cheesecake 116

Crispy Chocolate Ice Cream Mud Pie 136

D

Deep Dark Mousse 174

DESSERTS

Chocolate Cups with Lemon Cream 162

Chocolate Dream Cups 186

Chocolate Mini-Puffs 160

Chocolate Raspberry Dessert 182

Chocolate Syrup Swirl Dessert 168

Deep Dark Mousse 174

Easy Chocoberry Cream Dessert 180

Hot Chocolate Soufflé 176

Milk Chocolate Pots de Crème 166

MINI KISSES® BRAND Pumpkin Mousse Cups 234

Peanut Butter Fondue 172

Pears with Chocolate-Orange Sauce.............................. 190

SPECIAL DARK® Fudge Fondue....................................... 192

Toffee Bread Pudding with Cinnamon Toffee Sauce 198

Double Chocolate Coconut Oatmeal Cookies........................ 28

Double-Drizzled Chocolate Shortbread Cookies 20

Drinking Chocolate 240

E

Easy Chocoberry Cream Dessert 180

Easy Chocolate Cheesepie.. 154

Easy Chocolate Coconut Cream Pie....................................... 148

Easy Chocolate Cream-Filled Torte 196

Easy Easter KISSES® BRAND & Peanut Butter Cup Pie 230

English Toffee Bars 70

European Mocha Fudge Cake 82

F

Filled Chocolate Meringues.. 202

Five Layer Bars 56

Flourless Chocolate Torte.. 184

Fudge-Bottomed Chocolate Layer Pie 122

Fudgey Mocha Nut Pie 146

G

German Black Forest Cherry Torte 90

H

HERSHEY₅S Chocolate Peppermint Roll 248

HERSHEY₅S Cocoa Cream Pie... 156

HERSHEY₅S Double Chocolate MINI KISSES® BRAND Cookies.. 40

HERSHEY₅S KISSES® BRAND Birthday Cake 228

HERSHEY₅S Lavish Chocolate Cake 84

HERSHEY₅S "PERFECTLY CHOCOLATE" Chocolate Cake......... 100

HERSHEY₅S SPECIAL DARK® Chocolate Layered Cheesecake 110

HERSHEY₅S SPECIAL DARK® Snack Cake Medley 98

HERSHEY₅S SPECIAL DARK® Truffle Brownie Cheesecake 114

HERSHEY₅S White and Dark Chocolate Fudge Torte............ 178

Holiday Chocolate Cake 232

Holiday Coconut Cake.. 236

Holiday Double Peanut Butter Fudge Cookies 242

Holiday Fudge Torte 238

Holiday Red Raspberry Chocolate Bars 246

Hot Chocolate Soufflé 176

HUGS & KISSES® BRAND Crescents.. 188

K

KISSES® BRAND Fluted Cups with Peanut Butter Filling........... 218

KISSES® BRAND Macaroon Cookies... 30

M

Milk Chocolate Pots de Crème... 166

Mini Brownie Cups 18

Mini Chocolate Pies.. 150

MINI KISSES® BRAND Fruit Bars.. 52

MINI KISSES® BRAND Milk Chocolate Peanut Butter Cookies.. 22

MINI KISSES® BRAND Pumpkin Mousse Cups 234

Mocha Brownie Nut Torte 194

Mocha Molten Chocolate Cake... 78

P

Peanut Butter and Milk Chocolate Chip Cookie Pie 126

Peanut Butter Blossoms... 34

Peanut Butter Cut-Out Cookies 32

Peanut Butter Fondue 172

Peanut Butter Fudge Brownie Bars.. 50

Peanut Butter Glazed Chocolate Bars................................... 48

Peanut Butter Holiday Cheesecake...................................... 108

Pears with Chocolate-Orange Sauce.................................... 190

Pecan MINI KISSES® BRAND Cups.. 24

PIES

All-Chocolate Boston Cream Pie 124

Chocolate and Vanilla-Swirled Cheese Pie 128

Chocolate Chip Cookie Dough Cheesepie 134

Chocolate Magic Mousse Pie.. 140

Chocolate Marbled Peanut Butter Pie 138

index

Classic Boston Cream Pie 144

Classic Chocolate Cream Pie... 130

Crispy Chocolate Ice Cream Mud Pie 136

Easy Chocolate Cheesepie.. 154

Easy Chocolate Coconut Cream Pie.............................. 148

Easy Easter KISSES® BRAND & Peanut Butter Cup Pie 230

Fudge-Bottomed Chocolate Layer Pie 122

Fudgey Mocha Nut Pie.. 146

HERSHEY®S Cocoa Cream Pie 156

Mini Chocolate Pies 150

Peanut Butter and Milk Chocolate Chip Cookie Pie 126

REESE'S® Peanut Butter & HERSHEY®S
KISSES® BRAND Pie... 152

Upside-Down Hot Fudge Sundae Pie 142

White Chip Fruit Tart.. 132

R

REESE'S® Peanut Butter & HERSHEY®S
KISSES® BRAND Pie... 152

REESE'S® Peanut Butter Bark 204

Rich Cocoa Crinkle Cookies 36

S

Secret KISSES® BRAND Cookies.. 14

Shower Them with KISSES® BRAND Cake 244

SPECIAL DARK® Chocolate Chip Scones.............................. 226

SPECIAL DARK® Fudge Fondue.. 192

Strawberry Chocolate Chip Shortcake 96

T

Toffee Bread Pudding with Cinnamon Toffee Sauce........... 198

TORTES

Cherry-Glazed Chocolate Torte 164

Chocolate Almond Torte 94

Easy Chocolate Cream-Filled Torte 196

Flourless Chocolate Torte.. 184

German Black Forest Cherry Torte 90

HERSHEY®S White and Dark Chocolate
Fudge Torte 178

Holiday Fudge Torte 238

Mocha Brownie Nut Torte 194

Viennese Chocolate Torte 170

Triple Layer Cheesecake.. 112

U

Ultra Chocolate Cheesecake.. 118

Upside-Down Hot Fudge Sundae Pie................................... 142

V

Viennese Chocolate Torte.. 170

W

White & Chocolate Covered Strawberries........................... 212

White Chip Fruit Tart.. 132

metric conversion chart

VOLUME MEASUREMENTS (dry)

$\frac{1}{8}$ teaspoon = 0.5 mL
$\frac{1}{4}$ teaspoon = 1 mL
$\frac{1}{2}$ teaspoon = 2 mL
$\frac{3}{4}$ teaspoon = 4 mL
1 teaspoon = 5 mL
1 tablespoon = 15 mL
2 tablespoons = 30 mL
$\frac{1}{4}$ cup = 60 mL
$\frac{1}{3}$ cup = 75 mL
$\frac{1}{2}$ cup = 125 mL
$\frac{2}{3}$ cup = 150 mL
$\frac{3}{4}$ cup = 175 mL
1 cup = 250 mL
2 cups = 1 pint = 500 mL
3 cups = 750 mL
4 cups = 1 quart = 1 L

VOLUME MEASUREMENTS (fluid)

1 fluid ounce (2 tablespoons) = 30 mL
4 fluid ounces ($\frac{1}{2}$ cup) = 125 mL
8 fluid ounces (1 cup) = 250 mL
12 fluid ounces ($1\frac{1}{2}$ cups) = 375 mL
16 fluid ounces (2 cups) = 500 mL

WEIGHTS (mass)

$\frac{1}{2}$ ounce = 15 g
1 ounce = 30 g
3 ounces = 90 g
4 ounces = 120 g
8 ounces = 225 g
10 ounces = 285 g
12 ounces = 360 g
16 ounces = 1 pound = 450 g

DIMENSIONS

$\frac{1}{16}$ inch = 2 mm
$\frac{1}{8}$ inch = 3 mm
$\frac{1}{4}$ inch = 6 mm
$\frac{1}{2}$ inch = 1.5 cm
$\frac{3}{4}$ inch = 2 cm
1 inch = 2.5 cm

OVEN TEMPERATURES

250°F = 120°C
275°F = 140°C
300°F = 150°C
325°F = 160°C
350°F = 180°C
375°F = 190°C
400°F = 200°C
425°F = 220°C
450°F = 230°C

BAKING PAN SIZES

Utensil	Size in Inches/Quarts	Metric Volume	Size in Centimeters
Baking or Cake Pan (square or rectangular)	8×8×2	2 L	20×20×5
	9×9×2	2.5 L	23×23×5
	12×8×2	3 L	30×20×5
	13×9×2	3.5 L	33×23×5
Loaf Pan	8×4×3	1.5 L	20×10×7
	9×5×3	2 L	23×13×7
Round Layer Cake Pan	8×1½	1.2 L	20×4
	9×1½	1.5 L	23×4
Pie Plate	8×1¼	750 mL	20×3
	9×1¼	1 L	23×3
Baking Dish or Casserole	1 quart	1 L	—
	1½ quarts	1.5 L	—
	2 quarts	2 L	—